BRITISH MUSEUM
GUIDE & MAP

CONTENTS

From Steve Adamson 4/86

Inner Coffin of Henutmehit. From Thebes, about 1400 BC. Height 1.88m.

This Ticket entitles

to a Sight of the

BRITISH MUSEUM,

at the Hour of One on Wednesday

the 3 of March 1790.

No Money is to be given to the Servants.

INTRODUCTION

by the Director, Dr D. M. Wilson

The British Museum is unique. Behind its grand neo-classical façade lies one of the greatest storehouses of the world's treasures. It has more visitors than practically any other museum in the world – up to four million a year. It is a world within a world: it has its own publishing house, restaurants, security force, social workers, scientists, cleaners, teachers, engineers, and accountants. At base, however, it is a great collecting institution and the assembling, conservation and study of material is its central function.

Its founder was one of the greatest collectors of all time, Sir Hans Sloane, a fashionable physician in Queen Anne's London. Sloane assembled an immense private collection of plants, fossils, minerals, zoological, anatomical and pathological specimens, antiquities and artificial curiosities, prints, drawings, coins, books and manuscripts. When he died in 1753 at the age of ninety-two this collection, comprising some 80,000 objects, was by the terms of his will offered to the nation in return for the provision of a suitable repository and the payment of £20,000 to his heirs. An Act of Parliament was passed authorising the holding of a public lottery to raise the necessary money. Trustees, headed by the Archbishop of Canterbury, the Speaker of the House of Commons and the Lord Chancellor, were appointed to oversee the new Museum. (The British Museum was, with relatively minor amendments, governed by this Act until the passing of the new British Museum Act in 1963.) To the Sloane collection were added the great Cotton and Harley libraries and the institution was opened on 15 January 1759 in a decaying seventeenth-century mansion, Montagu House, which stood on the present site of the Museum. It was, and remains, a universal museum which covered the whole of human knowledge, by collecting both natural and artificial products. Although today the paintings, the library and the natural history collections have been removed elsewhere, its collections still span the globe.

Glimpses of the Museum's past. *CENTRE.* **Sir Hans Sloane, Bt. (1660–1753), founder of the British Museum; an early Admission Ticket, for which there was an ever-growing waiting list.** *LEFT. (top)* **the encampment in the Museum Gardens of a contingent of the York Regiment of Militia, sent down from Doncaster to protect the Museum and help control the mobs during the Gordon Riots of 1780;** *(centre)* **the stuffed giraffes at the top of Montagu House staircase, by George Scharf the Elder, *c.* 1845;** *(bottom)* **the south-west corner of Montagu House from Great Russell Street by the same artist, *c.* 1848–9.** *RIGHT. (top)* **the Egyptian Room in 1847;** *(centre)* **one of the colossal human-headed lions from Nineveh arrives at the Museum in 1852;** *(bottom)* **Montagu House, the original British Museum.**

The collections increased rapidly through the generosity of private benefactors and a sometimes reluctant government. In 1756 George II presented the old royal library of England and with it the privilege of copyright deposit, now transferred to the British Library. In 1802 the Rosetta Stone and other Egyptian antiquities were acquired from George III. Two great collections of classical sculptures – the so-called Townley and Elgin marbles, which largely conditioned English Classical taste of the early nineteenth century – also came to Bloomsbury.

Montagu House was soon bursting at the seams and the Trustees, with the assistance of a young architect Robert (later Sir Robert) Smirke, began to plan for expansion. Impetus was given to this when in 1823 George IV presented his father's magnificent library and Parliament voted funds to house it fittingly. The East Wing, including the great King's Library, was completed in 1827 and the building as it is today gradually arose over the next thirty years. In 1846 Robert Smirke retired and was succeeded by his younger brother Sydney. The domed Reading Room in the quadrangle, not part of the original design, was opened in 1857 and is Sydney Smirke's work.

The original division of the collections had been tripartite – Printed Books (including prints), Manuscripts (including coins and drawings) and Natural and Artificial Productions (everything else). The growing importance of the antiquities collections was recognised in 1807 by the establishment of a separate department. The Department of Prints and Drawings was set up in 1836 and in 1860, on the retirement of the eighty-year-old Keeper, Edward Hawkins, the antiquities department was split three ways – into Coins and Medals, Greek and Roman and Oriental. The latter included ethnography and medieval antiquities and is the ancestor of six present departments.

In the late nineteenth century and during the first decades of the twentieth century the collections increased prodigiously, often as a result of excavation and expeditions by scholars and explorers all over the world. Early emphasis had been on Classical and Biblical material and in 1834 there were practically no British antiquities in the Museum. By mid-century, however, this part of the collections was growing rapidly as a result of the new developments in European archaeology triggered off by Danish, French and English research. The overcrowding was relieved by moving the Natural History collections to South Kensington in the early 1880s. Further space was provided by the completion in 1884 of a wing to the east of the main block, and the King Edward VII galleries to the north were opened in 1914. The Duveen Gallery which houses the Elgin marbles was completed in 1938; its opening was, however, delayed for more than twenty years because of war damage. An administrative wing containing a special exhibition gallery and a public restaurant was opened in 1978.

In 1970 the ethnography collection moved to a temporary home at the Museum of Mankind in Burlington Gardens, off Piccadilly. In 1973 the three library departments were divorced from the Museum and, with other library organisations, formed a new body, the British Library; ultimately they will be gathered together in a new purpose-built building.

Although its collections are largely of the past, the British Museum has, at times unwillingly, always looked to the future. As the collections develop, visitors increase and display techniques change so that the 'old curiosity shop in Great Russell Street' changes too. 1981 saw the opening of a remodelled Egyptian Sculpture Gallery, much of the cost of which was met by private donations. The Wolfson Galleries (also made possible through the generosity of a private donor) will enable the public to see again the great Townley collection. Other major changes in galleries are being planned before the end of the century.

It is not possible within the scope of this brief guide to do full justice to the immense and varied collections of the Museum, but I hope it will give visitors an insight into what the Museum offers, and that they will return again to explore it further.

D. M. WILSON *Director*

opposite. **Shaping the Portland stone columns for the Colonnade, by George Scharf the Elder, *c.* 1845.**

below. **The Museum of Mankind at 6 Burlington Gardens.**

COINS AND MEDALS

The Department's extensive collection comprises coins of all periods and places from the seventh century BC to the present day, medals of all kinds including awards and decorations, tokens, coin weights, and paper money. The collection is not housed in display form within the Department, but it is available for consultation and study in a Students' Room. The regulations for admission to and use of the Students' Room can be obtained by application to the Department. General enquiries regarding coins, medals and paper money are also dealt with by members of the staff.

Exhibition Gallery
ROOM 50

This is devoted to 2,000 years of Coins and Medals in Great Britain. A guide to the exhibition is available.

The earliest coins in Britain were brought by people from Belgic Gaul; the types of the first coins used in this country were based on a gold stater of Philip II of Macedon (357–336 BC). The native British staters of

right

1 **Akragas, silver dekadrachm. c. 421 BC (rev.)**

2 **Second Jewish Revolt, silver shekel, AD 133–5 (obv.)**

3 **Carausius, aureus, AD 286–93 (obv.)**

4 **Henry VII, sovereign, 1489–1509 (obv. and rev.)**

5 **Charles I, triple unit, Oxford mint, 1644 (obv.)**

6 **James V of Scotland 'bonnet' piece, 1540 (obv.)**

7 **Mary, Queen of Scots, ryal, 1558 (obv.)**

8 **Kanishka, gold coin, c. AD 100 (rev.)**

9 **Mary I, portrait by Jacopo da Trezzi, 1555 (obv.)**

10 **Elizabeth I, Armada medal, 1588 (obv.)**

left. **Art Deco medal by André Lavrillier (1885–1958) in struck bronze, showing Leda and the Swan, 101 × 61 mm.**

1

2

3

4

5

6

7

8

9

10

the famous King Cunobeline carrying the names of himself and his capital Camulodunum (Colchester), ear-of-wheat and horse designs, are far more accomplished. For the four hundred years after the Roman conquest of Britain by the Emperor Claudius in AD 43, Roman coins circulated. Some of the earliest Anglo-Saxon coins, though about two centuries later than the end of Roman rule, are based on Roman prototypes. There is a good range of silver Anglo-Saxon pennies, and some rare gold ones, before the Norman conquest of William I in 1066. Some magnificent pieces show the relative economic stability of medieval England and its influence on continental Europe.

With the Renaissance comes the revival of true coin and medallic portraiture, seen first on the silver groat of Henry VII of 1503–4, and perhaps best exemplified in the magnificent gold medal of Elizabeth I made on the occasion of the defeat of the Spanish Armada in 1588. Until the seventeenth century coins were made by hand by the hammered process; after the Restoration of Charles II milled coinage was introduced in 1661, and all hammered coins finally removed from circulation in 1733. All reigns are represented by coins and medals and there are separate displays in the gallery of the coinage of Ireland and Scotland.

Other Displays

Small displays of relevant coins and medals will be found in the galleries of other departments: there are Greek coins in the Greek and Roman Life Room, and in ground floor galleries of the Greek and Roman Department; Roman coins in the Greek and Roman Life Room, and in the exhibition devoted to Augustus in Room 70; coins of Roman Britain, including gold solidi from the Water Newton Treasure Trove in the Roman Britain Room; coins from the Oxus treasure in the Iranian Room; Jewish coins in the Palestinian Room; Oriental coins in the Edward VII Gallery; Celtic coins in the Iron Age Gallery; and the seventh-century gold coins from the Sutton Hoo ship burial in the Early Medieval Room.

right

1 Nexos, silver tetradrachm, c. 460 BC

2 Claudius I, aureus, AD 46

3 Alfred the Great, silver penny, 871–99

4 Cunobelin, gold stater, AD 10–40

5 William I, silver penny, 1066–87

6 Edward III, gold noble, 1346–51

7 Edward IV, gold angel, 1471–83

8 Edward VI, silver crown, 1551

9 James I, gold laurel, 1618–25

10 George III, gold sovereign, 1820

11 Victoria, Gothic florin, 1852

12 Elizabeth II, silver crown, 1953

A selection of titles about the coins and medals collections available from the Museum Shop:

Ancient Greek Portrait Coins
IAN CARRADICE

Anglo-Saxon Pennies
MICHAEL DOLLEY

Coins of Greek Sicily
G. K. JENKINS

The Coins of Late Antiquity
ANDREW BURNETT

Coins of the Macedonians
MARTIN PRICE

The Coins of Roman Britain
ANDREW BURNETT

An Introduction to Celtic Coins
DEREK ALLEN

2000 Years of British Coins and Medals
JOHN KENT

The Art of the Medal
MARK JONES

1

2

3

4

5

6

7

8

9

10

11

12

EGYPTIAN ANTIQUITIES

The collections in the Department of Egyptian Antiquities represent all stages in the development of ancient Egyptian civilisation from the earliest times to the Christian era. The historical (Dynastic) period, which began about three thousand years before Christ, was preceded by a series of prehistoric (Predynastic) cultures which are well exemplified in the Department by groups of material acquired from the excavation of key sites. For the historical period, sculptures, paintings and objects of all kinds and of many materials illustrate the achievements of the Egyptians in art, craftsmanship, and industry. The large collection of papyri contains examples of most categories of ancient document. Religion and burial customs are represented in rich detail by the well preserved material derived from cemeteries and temples. The early Christian (Coptic) collection includes inscribed gravestones, textiles and ritual and domestic objects.

Rosetta Stone. *above.* **Discovered by the French in 1799 but ceded to Great Britain by the Treaty of Alexandria, this slab of black basalt is named from its find-place. The text, written in three scripts (hieroglyphs, demotic and Greek) but in only two languages (Egyptian and Greek), is a decree passed on 27 March 196 BC by assembled Egyptian priests conferring honours on King Ptolemy V in return for his services to Egypt. Height 1.14m.**

Fowling in the marshes. *left.* **Wall-painting from the tomb of Nebamun at Thebes (*c.* 1400 BC) showing him hunting birds with a throw-stick – a favourite pastime – accompanied by his wife, small daughter and house cat. Height 82cm.**

Egyptian Sculpture Gallery

ROOM 25

The nucleus of the great exhibition of sculptures seen in this gallery was a collection of large antiquities surrendered by the French at the Capitulation of Alexandria in 1801. At the southern entry to the gallery is the 'Rosetta Stone', a slab of black basalt inscribed with a decree dated to the ninth year of king Ptolemy V (Spring 196 BC) written in ancient Greek and in two forms of ancient Egyptian script: hieroglyphs or sacred writing and demotic or the people's writing. This bilingual inscription, discovered by the French at Rosetta in the western delta in 1799 and brought to England in 1802, was instrumental through its Greek section in providing a key to the decipherment of hieroglyphs, a script unread for 1400 years. The breakthrough came once it had been established that the elongated ovals called cartouches, which occur frequently in the hieroglyphic section, always contain the royal name.

The main exhibition is introduced by a pair of red granite reclining lions of Amenophis III, one of them later inscribed by Tutankhamun (*c.* 1355 BC). Thereafter the sculptures are arranged generally in order of date: an alabaster standing woman (*c.* 2450 BC); painted limestone figure of Nenkheftka, a Fifth Dynasty nobleman (*c.* 2400 BC); statues of king Sesostris III of the Twelfth Dynasty (*c.* 1850 BC); colossal limestone bust of Amenophis III (*c.* 1400 BC); partially gilded human-form coffin of Lady Henutmehit (*c.* 1400 BC); granite torsos of Ramesses II (*c.* 1250 BC); sphinx with the features of the Nubian king

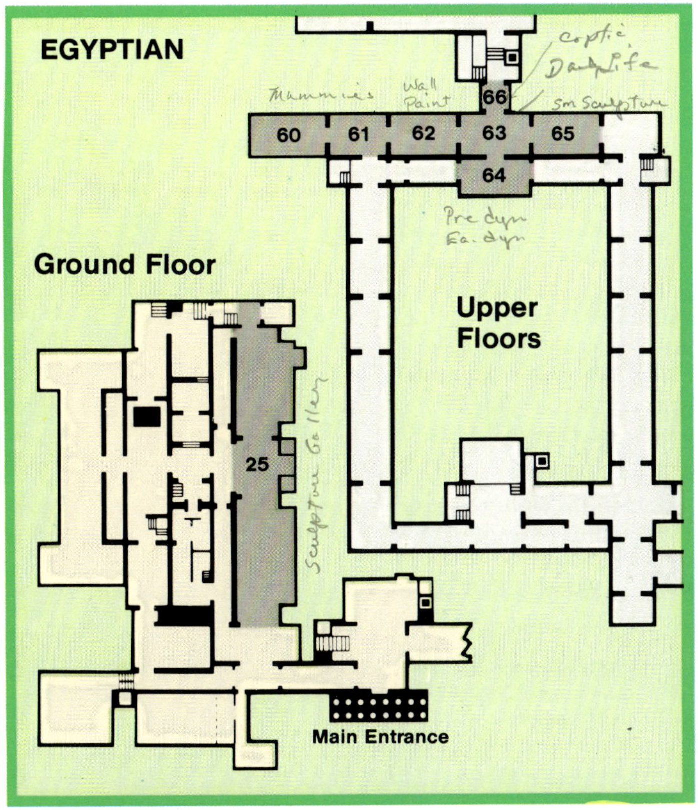

Body of predynastic man. Although he died before 3100 BC, 'Ginger' (named from the colour of his hair) has been perfectly preserved by the hot dry desert sand in which he was buried at Gebelein. As in other contemporary burials, before mummification was practised, his body lies curled up on its left side surrounded by black-topped red pots to contain food and drink to sustain the spirit forms released at death on their long journey through the Underworld to the Egyptian heaven. His flint knives were for use in the Other World. Length 1.63 m.

Taharqa (*c.* 680 BC); massive granite sarcophagus of Nectanebo II, Egypt's last native pharaoh (*c.* 345 BC). The Gallery also contains many funerary and dedicatory stelae and architectural elements from tombs and temples including false doors and offering tables, columns, small obelisks and a shrine. Of interest is the false door of the nobleman Ptahshepses (*c.* 2520–2435 BC) who lived under at least eight pharaohs; the stela of the official Tjetji (*c.* 2100 BC) gives information on the period of civil war

Ramesses II, upper part of colossus. **Two differently coloured granites have been used to best advantage in this torso from Ramesses' funerary temple at Thebes, *c.* 1250 BC. It was transported by G. Belzoni, circus strongman turned archaeologist, who obtained many of the Museum's first Egyptian sculptures. Shelley used its features as a model when writing 'Ozymandias' about another of Ramesses' colossi which is still in Egypt. Height 2.67m.**

at the end of the First Intermediate Period; a damaged basalt slab called the Shabaka Stone (*c.* 710 BC) is inscribed with a Twenty-fifth Dynasty copy of an earlier account of the Memphite Creation legend.

First and Second Egyptian Rooms

ROOMS 60/61

Exhibited here are mummies and mummy cases, mummy masks and wooden coffins, equipment used by embalmers and the priests who ritually revivified the mummy before it was sealed in the tomb, and Canopic boxes and jars which once contained the embalmed internal organs removed from the corpse during mummification. Of special interest is the sand-dried, naturally preserved body of 'Ginger', a man of the Predynastic Period who died over five thousand years ago; mummies of sacred animals including cats, crocodiles, hawks, gazelles and baboons reveal Egyptian reverence for certain living creatures as being earthly manifestations of the gods; declining standards are evident in the heavily bandaged mummy of Cleopatra, a Roman official's daughter (*c.* 110 AD), with scenes crudely painted directly on the linen; rectangular wooden coffins of Middle Kingdom date (*c.* 2000 BC) have maps of the Underworld and the two paths to Heaven on their floors.

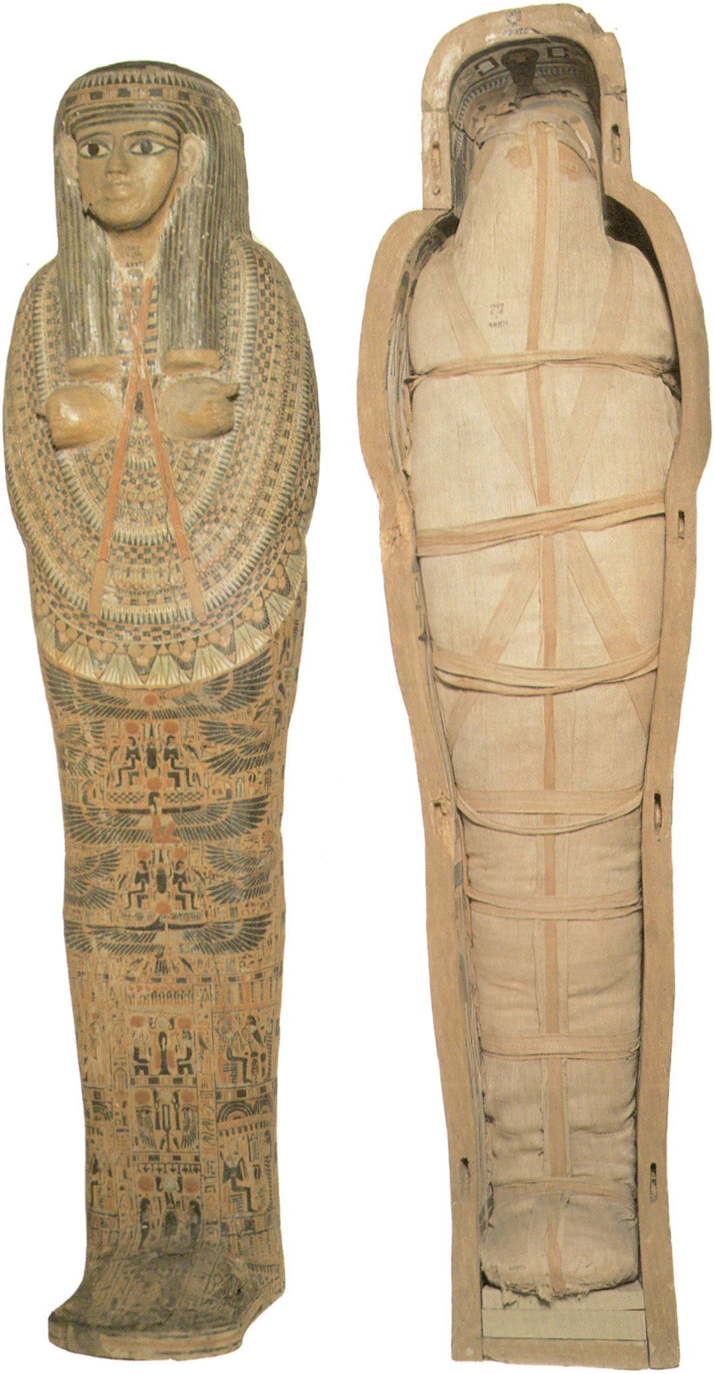

Mummy and coffin of priestess. This superbly wrapped mummy from Thebes of 21st Dynasty date (*c.* 1000 BC), with intricately arranged coloured linen strips holding the shrouds in place, exemplifies the peak of the embalmers' art. The human-form wooden coffin with brightly painted funerary scenes on moulded plaster, heavy floral shawl covering the breast and crossed red braces, are typical of the period. Length 1.64m.

Third Egyptian Room

ROOM 62

Best-known of the wall-paintings from private tombs, generally of

Eighteenth Dynasty date (*c.* 1400 BC), exhibited in this room are 'Garden pool with trees' and 'Counting geese and cattle'. From royal tombs at Thebes come curious wooden figures of animal-headed Underworld deities. Numerous *shabti*-figures, some still packed in *shabti*-boxes, represent tiny servants of the deceased, usually carrying agricultural implements and bearing the spell which will bring them to life to work for their dead owner in the Other World. One of the most interesting of many amulets from mummy wrappings is a human-head green jasper Heart Scarab set in gold belonging to king Sobkemsaf II (*c.* 1640 BC) which is known to have been stolen by ancient tomb robbers in *c.* 1125 BC but did not enter the collection until three thousand years later. The exhibition of papyri in this room includes various editions of the Book of the Dead (collections of spells to enable the deceased to pass safely through the Underworld to Heaven), ranging in date from the Eighteenth Dynasty to the second century AD. These were specially chosen for their illustrations, called vignettes, among which those of Ani, Hunefer and Nesitanebtasheru have particularly fine representations of the Weighing of the Heart, Underworld regions and inhabitants, funeral and agricultural activities in the Fields of Ialu. Other papyri in this room are non-funerary and illustrate in hieratic and demotic scripts every type of text including temple archives, private letters, legal documents, wisdom books, medical treatises, mathematical text books and literary works. Especially interesting are the Abusir temple accounts which form the earliest surviving body

of written papyri (*c.* 2400 BC), the will of Lady Neskhons (265 BC), the Rhind mathematical papyrus (*c.* 1580 BC), the Battle of Kadesh poem (*c.* 1250 BC) and an account of a tomb robbers' trial (*c.* 1130 BC).

Fourth Egyptian Room

ROOM 63

Exhibits here are devoted to demonstrating aspects of daily life among the Egyptians and include clothing and basketry, cosmetic items, musical instruments, toys and games, furniture, stone vessels, tools, weapons and household utensils, weights and measures, real food from tombs (dried fish, fruit, duck, bread), wooden model servants to provide food and drink in the Other World and model boats to provide transport.

Fifth Egyptian Room

ROOM 65

Small sculptures in stone, wood and metal, small objects of ivory and bone, small figured reliefs and statuettes of gods and sacred animals are exhibited here. Particularly interesting are

Votive hollow-cast bronze cat wearing earrings. The animal is sacred to the goddess Bastet; Saite Period, after 600 BC. Height 16.5 cm.

Queen Ahmes-Nefertari. *left.* **Wall-painting from the tomb of Kynebu at Thebes (*c.* 1150 BC) showing the deified mother of King Amenophis I of the 18th Dynasty who with her son became the patrons of the necropolis-workers at Deir el-Medina. Height 43 cm.**

Glass fish. *below.* **Cosmetic vessel from el-Amarna *c.* 1370 BC shaped like a *bulti*, made of core-built blue glass with trailed festoon decorations. Length 14.5 cm.**

Model boat. *above.* Wooden funerary vessel of the 12th Dynasty, *c.* 1850 BC, with protective ***udjats*** on prow and paddles, showing the mummy on an animal-footed bier beneath a lotus-pillared canopy flanked by female mourners. Length 66.7 cm.

Agricultural scenes from Book of the Dead Papyrus. *below.* The High Priestess Anhai, *c.* 1100 BC, accompanied by her husband pulls flax, cuts emmer and ploughs the earth in the presence of various benevolent inhabitants of the Fields of Ialu, the Egyptian paradise. Height 42 cm.

bronze votive cats (after 600 BC), sculptures and reliefs of king Akhenaten and his family in the Amarna style of art (*c.* 1370 BC) and the granite Benson head (*c.* 600 BC).

Sixth Egyptian Room

ROOM 64

This is devoted principally to objects of Predynastic and Early Dynastic date, pottery of all periods, scarabs, jewellery, glass and glazed composition. Some of the most interesting pieces are the Pitt-Rivers knife (*c.* 3200 BC), large commemorative scarabs of Amenophis III (*c.* 1400 BC), polychrome glass cosmetic vessels (*c.* 1400 BC), the earliest Egyptian models of the human form (*c.* 4000 BC), a Predynastic diadem of gold and precious stones (*c.* 3200 BC).

Coptic Corridor

ROOM 66

This is devoted to portraits of the Roman Period modelled in plaster or painted in coloured wax on wooden boards (the wax portrait of Artemidorus, *c.* second century AD, is rather fine), carved stonework in which ancient Egyptian, Classical and Christian elements have been united, and textiles, jewellery and ritual objects dating from the first to ninth centuries AD.

A selection of titles about the Egyptian collections available from the Museum Shop:

An Introduction to Ancient Egypt
T. G. H. JAMES

Egyptian Sculpture
T. G. H. JAMES AND W. V. DAVIS

The British Museum and Ancient Egypt
T. G. H. JAMES

The Rosetta Stone
CAROL ANDREWS

Mummy portrait of a woman. Greek inhabitant of Egypt painted in coloured wax on a cedar wood panel for insertion in wrappings over mummy's face. From Saqqara, 2nd century AD. Height 37 cm.

Pair of bracelets. Gold with lapis lazuli and glass inlays showing Harpocrates seated; inscribed for Nemareth, son of King Sheshonq I of the 22nd Dynasty, *c.* 940 BC. Height 4.2 cm.

GREEK AND ROMAN ANTIQUITIES

The ground floor galleries of the Department illustrate the development of Greek art from the Bronze Age (beginning about 3000 BC) to the Roman Empire. Below are displays of Greek and Roman architecture and of Latin and Greek inscriptions. The upper galleries are being redesigned but include the old Terracotta and Bronze Gallery, the Daily Life Room, the Greek Vase Collection and a new exhibition of Roman portraits. The Students' Room is open by appointment for private research.

The ground floor exhibition starts beyond the bookstall gallery. Two half-columns from the so-called 'Treasury of Atreus' at Mycenae, a royal tomb of the thirteenth century BC, flank the doorway to the first room.

Cycladic Room
ROOM 1

Artefacts from the distinctive culture that flourished in the Cycladic Islands about 3200 to 2000 BC include marble vessels and figurines of women with folded arms.

Greek Bronze Age Room 3000 to 1000 BC
ROOM 2

Material from Minoan Crete includes pottery and statuettes, among which a group of a bull and an acrobat is noteworthy, gold jewellery from the 'Aegina Treasure', and a storage-jar (pithos) from Knossos. In addition to sculpture and decorative stonework from the Treasury of Atreus at Mycenae there are Mycenaean weapons and pottery and separate displays of Mycenaean antiquities from the islands of Rhodes and Cyprus.

Archaic Greek Room 1000 to 500 BC
ROOM 3

This room is best visited clockwise. In the Dark Ages after the fall of the Mycenaean Empire the Greeks produced pottery with geometric decoration and charming bronze statuettes of animals, especially horses. Renewed trade with the East reintroduced Greek craftsmen to oriental themes including imaginary animals like the griffin, here portrayed in pottery and bronze. Greek sculptors and painters concentrated on the representation of the human figure and the new prosperity encouraged the manufacture of statuettes and gold jewellery. The alphabet allowed artists to explain their subject (e.g. Hector, Menelaus and Euphorbos on a Rhodian plate) and to sign their works (vases by Sophilos and Exekias). Stone sculpture includes fragments from the archaic Temple of Artemis at

above. 'The Aegina Treasure' included this gold ornament. It shows the so-called 'Master of Animals', a nature-god, whose Cretan name is not known. Wearing a Cretan belt and loincloth, an elaborate headdress and earrings, he stands amid lotus buds holding a goose in each hand. Although found on Aegina, it was made in Crete about 1600 BC. Height 6 cm.

Marble Cycladic 'Idol'. *left.* **Female figurines were often placed in tombs on the Cycladic Islands between 3200 and 2000 BC, but in the absence of written records their purpose and meaning remain mysterious. Their simplified forms, especially the straight sided groove between the legs, reflect the use of abrasives like emery in their manufacture, iron tools being still unknown. Height 49 cm.**

Ephesus and seated figures from Didyma near Miletus.

Room of the Kouroi

ROOM 4

Two marble statues of naked youths (*kouroi*) come from Boeotia and Cyprus. A third example (the Strangford Kouros) is shown in Room 5.

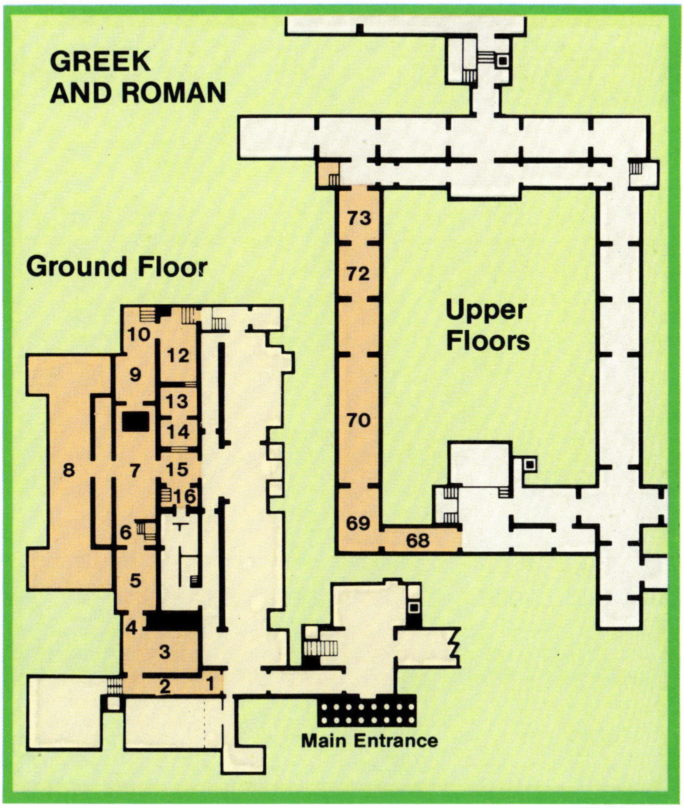

Room of the Harpy Tomb

ROOM 5

The development of Greek art from about 500 to 440 BC can be seen in four groups of showcases, best studied in sequence. In the first group are Athenian vases signed by Epiktetos, terracotta figures from Boeotia and a bronze statuette of a girl runner, perhaps Spartan. Around 490 to 470 vases by Douris, Makron and the Berlin Painter are especially noteworthy. Bronze mirrors supported by female statuettes were long in fashion, and examples from different periods are shown. A splendid cup with Aphrodite riding a goose, painted in outline and wash on a white ground, was made around 460 BC. The white-ground technique was especially popular for *lekythoi* (perfume-bottles) intended for use at funerals. Important sculptures on a large scale include the head of a bronze statue from Cyprus and stone reliefs from Xanthos in Lycia, especially the Harpy Tomb.

A staircase leads to the

Bassae Room

ROOM 6

The marble frieze from the Temple of Apollo at Bassae, carved towards 400 BC, illustrates the fight between Greeks and Centaurs and a battle of Herakles and other Greeks against the Amazons.

About 490–480 BC the Athenian vase-painter Makron decorated this red-figured *skyphos* (wine cup, 21.2 cm high): Triptolemos in his winged car carries corn as a gift to mankind from Demeter.

Nereid Room

ROOM 7

This large room contains the reconstructed façade of the Nereid Monument, named for the statues that stand between columns, formerly thought to be Nereids, but now usually identified as *Aurai* (Breezes). Built about 400 BC in the form of an Ionic temple on a high podium, it was the tomb of one of the rulers of Xanthos. The sculptured friezes include scenes of royal life: the siege of a city, a sacrifice, hunting and feasting.

Duveen Gallery

ROOM 8

This gallery houses the sculptures of the Parthenon, brought to England by Lord Elgin. On the left of the entrance is an introductory gallery. A tape-recorded tour may be hired. Built on the summit of the Acropolis in Athens between 447 and 432 BC, the Parthenon was richly ornamented with sculptures. Inside the colonnade was the great frieze, traditionally interpreted as the Panathenaic procession but now thought to show the presentation of the heroes of the battle of Marathon (490 BC) to the Olympian gods. This is now exhibited in the central gallery, with sculptures from the outside of the Parthenon in the transepts at either end. Fifteen square panels, or metopes, showing the struggle between Greeks and Centaurs came from the south side of the Temple. Altogether ninety-two metopes illustrated various mythological conflicts that symbolise the victories of Athens in the Persian Wars.

In the triangular gable, or pediment, at the west end of the Parthenon was a group of statues representing the contest between Athena and Poseidon for the land of Attica. Most of the surviving statues are fragmentary. The central group of the east pediment, representing the birth of Athena, has long been lost. The surviving figures are various divinities and chariot groups representing the sun and moon.

Room of the Caryatid

ROOM 9

The Athenian temple known as the Erechtheion was finished in 409 BC. The Caryatid is one of six female figures that stood for columns in the 'Porch of the

Two marble statues of young women show contrasts of style and function. The Caryatid from the Erechtheion at Athens (*left*, 2.51 m high) stands firm. Her drapery lies close to her breast and bent knee, revealing the forms, but over her straight right leg deep folds recall the fluting of the column that she replaces. The personified Breeze (*above*, 1.41 m high as preserved) stood with others between the columns of the Nereid Monument at Xanthos. She skims over waves (symbolised by a sea-bird) and her damp clothing appears almost transparent where it clings to her body.

Maidens'. A column from the east porch is shown opposite, near an inscription recording the building's progress. Also exhibited are the friezes from the Temple of Athena Nike and marble grave-reliefs. The showcases contain smaller objects of the late fifth and fourth centuries BC, including a hydria signed by Meidias, a bronze mirror showing Aphrodite and Pan and a rare wooden panel-painting of a seated goddess.

Payava Room

ROOM 10

The room is dominated by the Tomb of Payava from Xanthos, decorated with scenes from Payava's career. The showcases contain pottery, terracotta and bronzes manufactured in the Greek cities of Southern Italy. Particularly fine are the 'Siris Bronzes', decorated shoulder-straps from a breastplate. A very impressive life-size bronze portrait of a North African has eyes, lips and teeth inlaid (about 350 BC).

A staircase leads up to a balcony, giving a good view of the upper part of the tomb of Payava.

Etruscan Room

ROOM 11

The room contains a temporary exhibition of Etruscan sculpture, pottery, metalwork (including jewellery of very fine workmanship) and paintings. The terracotta sarcophagus of Seianti is particularly striking.

Mausoleum Room

ROOM 12

The Mausoleum at Halicarnassus was the tomb of Mausolos (died 353 BC), numbered among the Seven Wonders of the World on account of its architectural daring and its rich sculptural decoration. This included a frieze of the battle of Greeks and Amazons, colossal portrait statues and, on the apex of the building, a four-horse chariot (part of one horse is exhibited). From another of the Seven Wonders, the Temple of Artemis at Ephesus, comes one of its famous sculptured column-drums.

The staircase in the corner leads down to the

Room of Greek and Roman Architecture

The Doric, Ionic and Corinthian orders are represented by fragments of buildings from Greece, Asia Minor and other parts of the ancient world.

Room of Latin and Greek Inscriptions

A selection of public and private inscriptions on stone includes decrees from Athens and other Greek cities, Alexander the Great's dedication of a temple at Priene, and epitaphs in both Greek and Latin.

Hellenistic Room

ROOM 13

Near the entrance from Room 12 is the Demeter of

far left. The Parthenon Frieze (1.1 m high and originally about 160 m long) shows a procession that includes cavalry, chariots, animals for sacrifice, musicians, elders and maidens approaching twelve seated gods and goddesses. The procession resembles one that brought a new robe to the statue of Athena at the Panathenaic Festival, commemorating Athena's birthday. Differences between the Frieze and ancient descriptions of the Panathenaic procession have caused some scholars to believe that the Frieze shows the heroes of the Battle of Marathon being presented to the gods. These two young riders would then represent Athenians who died to secure their city's freedom in 490 BC.

left. This colossal marble horse (about 3 m high as preserved) was one of four that stood harnessed to a chariot on the apex of the Mausoleum or tomb of Mausolus at Halicarnassus.

below. The name of Seianti Thanunia Tlesnasa appears on this Etruscan sarcophagus of painted terracotta (1.22 m high, 2nd century BC), and her effigy appears on the lid. In her left hand she holds a bronze mirror and with her right she lifts her veil, in the traditional gesture of a bride.

Cnidus, a marble statue of the goddess seated on a throne. Other important marble sculptures are the head of Asclepius from Melos and the relief of the Apotheosis of Homer signed by Archelaos of Priene. In the showcases are delicate terracotta statues of 'Tanagra' type, a bowl with gold leaf decoration sandwiched between two layers of glass, an ivory statuette of a hunchback and a bronze head of a young African woman serving as a jug. Larger bronzes include the head of a goddess and a portrait of Sophocles.

First Roman Room

ROOM 14

Pride of place is given to the Portland Vase, a jar of blue and white glass with scenes illustrating the story of Peleus and his immortal bride Thetis. Most of the outer layer has been cut away leaving white figures on a blue ground, an effect imitated by Wedgwood. In the other showcases are displays of Roman pottery and glass as well as more expensive vessels in gold and silver, including part of the Chaourse Treasure. The Macon Treasure is represented by nine silver statuettes. Other small-scale sculptures include bronze statuettes of Jupiter and Mercury, a small marble figure

Atalanta is identified by the inscription (incomplete) on this mosaic from a Roman villa at Halicarnassus. Height 1.40m.

The Portland Vase *(above,* **25 cm high) owes its modern name to the 18th-century Duchess of Portland who acquired it in 1785 from Sir William Hamilton. A blue jasperware copy by Wedgwood is exhibited in Room 47.**

of Socrates and terracottas from Greece, Asia Minor and North Africa. Wall-paintings excavated near Pompeii illustrate the stories of Icarus and Ulysses. The statue of Apollo was excavated in the Temple of Apollo at Cyrene.

Second Roman Room

ROOM 15

Roman portraits include the Emperors Trajan (AD 98–117) and Antoninus Pius (AD 138–161). Noteworthy among the decorative sculptures are copies made for Roman patrons of Greek statues of athletes.

Northwest Staircase

A selection of Roman mosaics, chiefly from Asia Minor and North Africa, includes hunting and fishing scenes as well as mythological figures like Atalanta.

THE WOLFSON GALLERIES OF CLASSICAL SCULPTURES AND INSCRIPTIONS ROOMS 78–89

These galleries contain a wide range of Greek and Roman sculptures and a selection of Latin and Greek inscriptions (Room 78) including a temple-dedication by Alexander the Great.

Rooms 79–81 contain large numbers of funerary monuments, which reflect the status and taste of private individuals in many lands around the eastern Mediterranean. Room 80 includes a series of seated figures that once lined the Sacred Way leading to the oracular sanctuary of Apollo at Didyma in western Asia Minor. In Room 81 are more sculptures from the Mausoleum at Halicarnassus and the last temple of Artemis at Ephesus (see also Room 12). Fragments of sculpture from an earlier temple of Artemis on the same site are shown in Room 82.

Roman sculptures are shown in Rooms 83–85. They include sarcophagi and statues, in particular a series from Cyrene and a colossal portrait-head of the Empress Faustina. Room 84 is devoted to the sculptures collected in the later eighteenth century by Charles Townley, including his famous copy of Myron's Discus-thrower and the 'Townley Venus' from Ostia. In Room 85 are heads from statues of deities and heroes as well as sculptured portraits of Roman Emperors and distinguished Roman Citizens.

UPPER GALLERIES

Terracotta and Bronze Room

ROOM 68

A selection of small-scale sculptures in terracotta and bronze from various parts of the Greek and Roman world includes Etruscan and Sardinian bronzes.

Daily Life Room

ROOM 69

There are displays of glass, silver and jewellery in addition to an exhibition on various aspects of daily life in ancient Greece and Rome, such as warfare, athletics, agriculture, commerce, religion, education and housing.

Third Roman Room

ROOM 70

A new exhibition on 'The Image of Augustus' shows how the portraits of the first Roman Emperor were used as an instrument of propaganda. The story of Roman portraits is continued in an adjacent corridor (visitors approaching through this corridor should go straight through the Augustus exhibition and work back).

Greek Vase Room

ROOM 72

A temporary display of many of the vases from the Museum's collection, one of the largest and most comprehensive in the world.

A selection of titles about the Greek and Roman collections available from the Museum Shop:

Cypriote art in the British Museum
B. F. COOK (EDITOR)

The Elgin Marbles
B. F. COOK

Greek and Roman Art in the British Museum
B. F. COOK

Greek and Roman Life
IAN JENKINS

Greek Vases
DYFRI WILLIAMS

Memorials to the Roman Dead
SUSAN WALKER

The Townley Marbles
B. F. COOK

MEDIEVAL AND LATER ANTIQUITIES

Knight from the Lewis Chessmen. One of the 12th-century Scandinavian walrus ivory chessmen discovered on the Isle of Lewis in 1831 (available in replica). Height 10 cm.

Royal Gold Cup of the Kings of France and England, *c.* 1370–80. Height 23.6 cm.

The Department of Medieval and Later Antiquities is concerned with the art and archaeology of Europe and certain other Christian and Jewish cultures, from the Early Christian period right up to the twentieth century. Only a small proportion of the collections can be displayed in the public galleries, but objects not on display can be seen by appointment in the departmental students' room, or, for clocks and watches, the special Horological Students' Room.

The Lycurgus Cup. A late Roman cage-cup (*c.* AD 400) carved from a single block of pea-green glass, which turns a rich, wine red in transmitted light. The exquisitely fine carving shows the legendary Thracian king Lycurgus enmeshed by a vengeful vine. Height 20 cm.

The Early Medieval Room

ROOM 41

This room is in the process of reorganisation; when re-opened it will show objects spanning the years between the beginning of the fourth and the end of the eleventh centuries. Among the most important objects are the Lycurgus Cup, a remarkable late-Roman glass vessel of the fourth century AD; early Christian ivories and silver treasures; and the Franks Casket, an eighth-century Northumbrian whale's bone box carved with runic inscriptions and lively representations of Germanic folklore and scenes from Roman history and the Bible. The Early Medieval Room will also house the seventh-century finds from the Anglo-Saxon royal ship burial at Sutton Hoo in Suffolk, the most important Germanic grave found in Europe: the Sutton Hoo material is temporarily displayed in room 71.

The Medieval Room

ROOM 42

This contains antiquities of the Byzantine, Carolingian, Romanesque and Gothic periods, dating from between the ninth and the fifteenth centuries. To the right can be seen the Lothar crystal, a Carolingian engraved rock-crystal of the ninth century. To the left are the Lewis chessmen, carved from walrus ivory and found in 1831 on the isle of Lewis off the west coast of Scotland. In the centre of the room

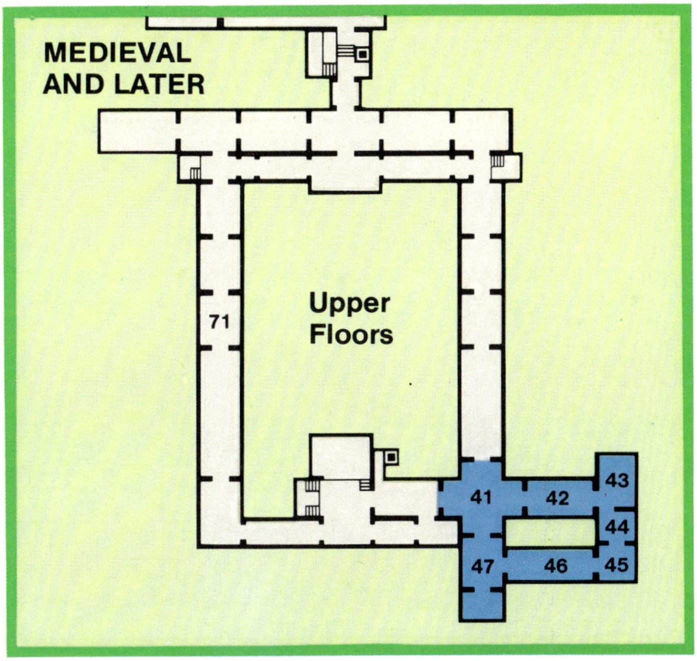

The Franks Casket. *right above.*
A Northumbrian whale's bone casket of the 8th century. Length 22.9cm.

Sutton Hoo Clasp. *right below.*
7th century. Richly decorated with *cloisonné* garnets and millefiori glass set in gold. Height 11.3cm.

The Lyte Jewel. This enamelled gold locket, containing a miniature of King James I by Nicholas Hilliard, was presented by the King to Thomas Lyte, a gentleman of Somerset, in 1610, as a reward for drawing up a pedigree to demonstrate that the royal ancestry could be traced back to the legendary founder of the British nation, Brut (or Brutus the Trojan). The hinged cover of the locket has an openwork design incorporating the monogram IR (IACOBUS REX), and is made of gold and enamel and set with diamonds. Length 7.9 cm.

are the mid-fourteenth-century paintings from St Stephen's Chapel, Westminster; near them are the medieval inlaid tiles from Chertsey Abbey. Standing cases show the royal gittern, the only major English musical instrument of the Middle Ages surviving, and the Royal Gold Cup of the Kings of England and France, one of the outstanding possessions of the Museum. To the right, the Savernake Horn and the fifteenth-century Flemish painted shield of parade are the outstanding objects in a display illustrating medieval secular life.

The Medieval Tile and Pottery Room

ROOM 43

Here the display is centred on the Canynges pavement from Bristol, dating from *c.* 1461. The cases nearby show medieval pottery of everyday use, while the panels above are inset with further examples of decorated medieval tiles, including the mid-thirteenth-century circular pavement from Henry III's chapel at Clarendon Palace, Wiltshire, above the kiln in which it was fired.

Gallery of Clocks and Watches

ROOM 44

The exhibition has been designed to show the major developments of mechanical timekeeping in Europe from the Middle Ages to the beginning of this century. Included is a spectacular *nef*, or ship-clock, of the late sixteenth century.

The Waddesdon Bequest Room

ROOM 45

This houses the single collection of medieval and Renaissance treasures bequeathed by Baron

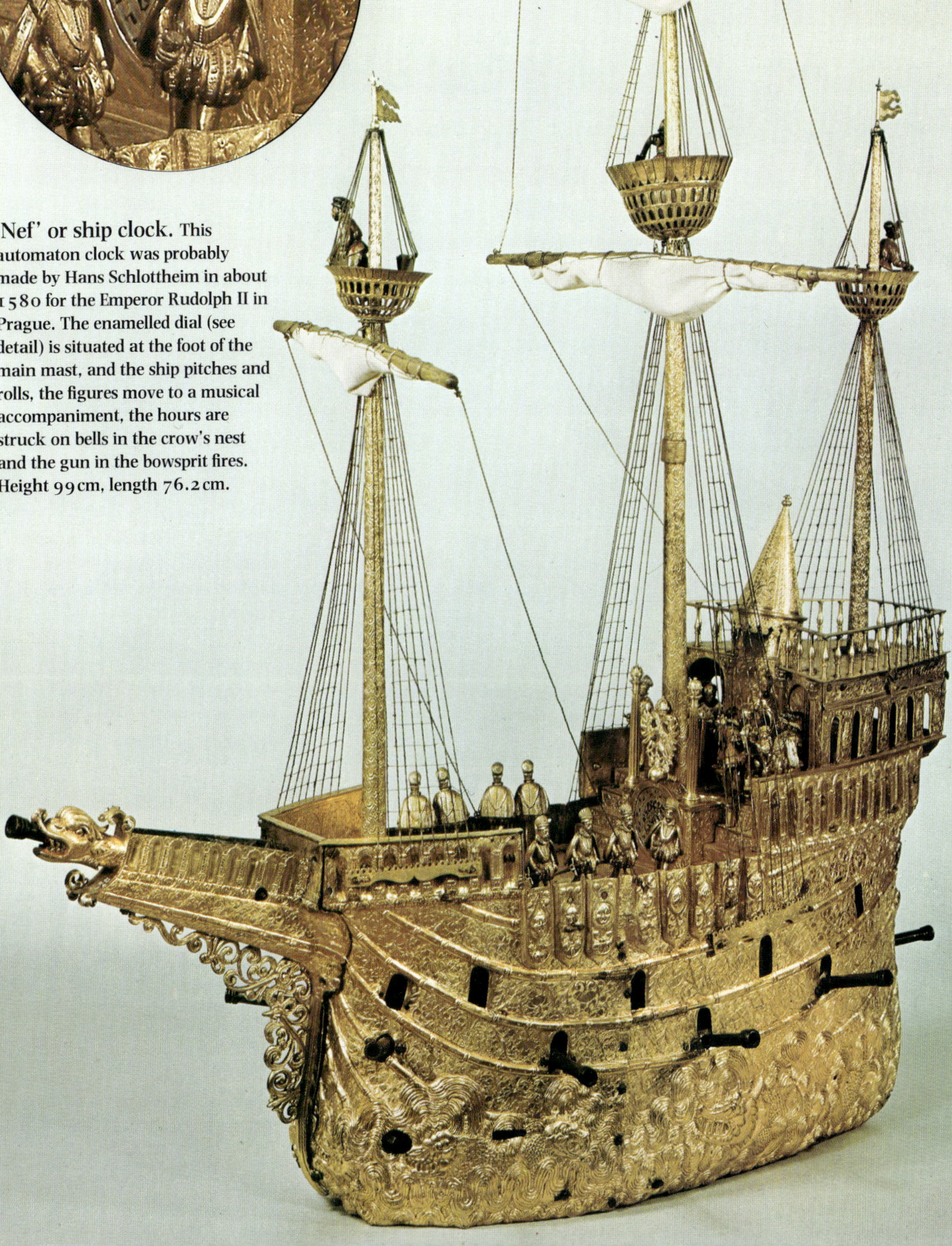

'Nef' or ship clock. This automaton clock was probably made by Hans Schlottheim in about 1580 for the Emperor Rudolph II in Prague. The enamelled dial (see detail) is situated at the foot of the main mast, and the ship pitches and rolls, the figures move to a musical accompaniment, the hours are struck on bells in the crow's nest and the gun in the bowsprit fires. Height 99 cm, length 76.2 cm.

Ferdinand de Rothschild in 1898. Dominated by goldsmiths' work, the room reflects the taste for lavish patronage of the arts, ostentatious wealth, the love of fine craftsmanship and of the curious, which were hallmarks of so many of the Renaissance courts.

The Renaissance Corridor

ROOM 46

In the corridor leaving the Waddesdon Room are objects from the Renaissance to the eighteenth century – European on the left, British on the right. There are a number of outstanding objects of historical and personal association, such as the signet ring of Mary, Queen of Scots and the silver seal-dies of Sir Walter Raleigh. A fine collection of Huguenot silver is displayed towards the end of the corridor on the left.

Bust of Prince Rupert.
above. **This life-size bust was made of salt-glazed stoneware, with touches of gilding, by John Dwight of London in about 1650. The Prince is wearing the collar and 'Great George' of the Order of the Garter. Height 61 cm.**

Pegasus Vase.
right. **1785. Josiah Wedgwood called this jasperware vase, taking its name from the flying horse on the lid, 'the finest and most perfect I have ever made'. He presented it to the Museum in 1786. Height 46.4cm.**

Renaissance and Later Room

ROOM 47

This room contains the magnificent Gift of jewellery from Professor and Mrs Hull Grundy. There is also a display of choice examples of pottery, porcelain and glass.

A selection of titles about the medieval and post-medieval collections available from the Museum Shop:

Clocks and Watches
HUGH TAIT

The Jeweller's Art
HUGH TAIT AND CHARLOTTE GERE

The Lewis Chessmen
MICHAEL TAYLOR

The Sutton Hoo Ship Burial: a handbook
RUPERT BRUCE-MITFORD

Mosaic brooch. *above. c.* 1860. By the Italian firm of Castellani. Diameter 5.3 cm.

Venetian glass goblet. *right. c.* 1450. Enamelled blue glass. Height 22.3 cm.

Maiolica dish from Faenza. *below. c.* 1510. The Death of the Virgin. Diameter 26.4 cm.

EGYPTIAN

- 25 Egyptian Sculpture
- 60/61 Mummies
- 62 Tomb paintings and papyri
- 63 Daily life in Ancient Egypt
- 64 Pottery and small objects
- 65 Small sculpture
- 66 Coptic Art

GREEK AND ROMAN

- 1 Cycladic Art
- 2 Greek Bronze Age
- 3 Archaic Greece
- 4 Room of the Kouroi
- 5 Room of the Harpy Tomb
- 6 Bassae Room
- 7 Nereid Room
- 8 Sculptures from the Parthenon (Elgin Marbles)
- 9 Caryatid Room
- 10 Payava Room
- 11 Etruscan Art (from stairs at 23)
- 12 Mausoleum Room
- 13 Hellenistic Art
- 14/15 Roman Art
- 22 Stairs down to Greek and Roman architecture and inscription room
- 23 Stairs to Etruscan Art
- 68 Greek and Roman bronzes and terracottas
- 69 Greek and Roman Life Room
- 70 Roman portraits
- 71 Sutton Hoo Ship Burial *
- 72/73 Greek vase rooms

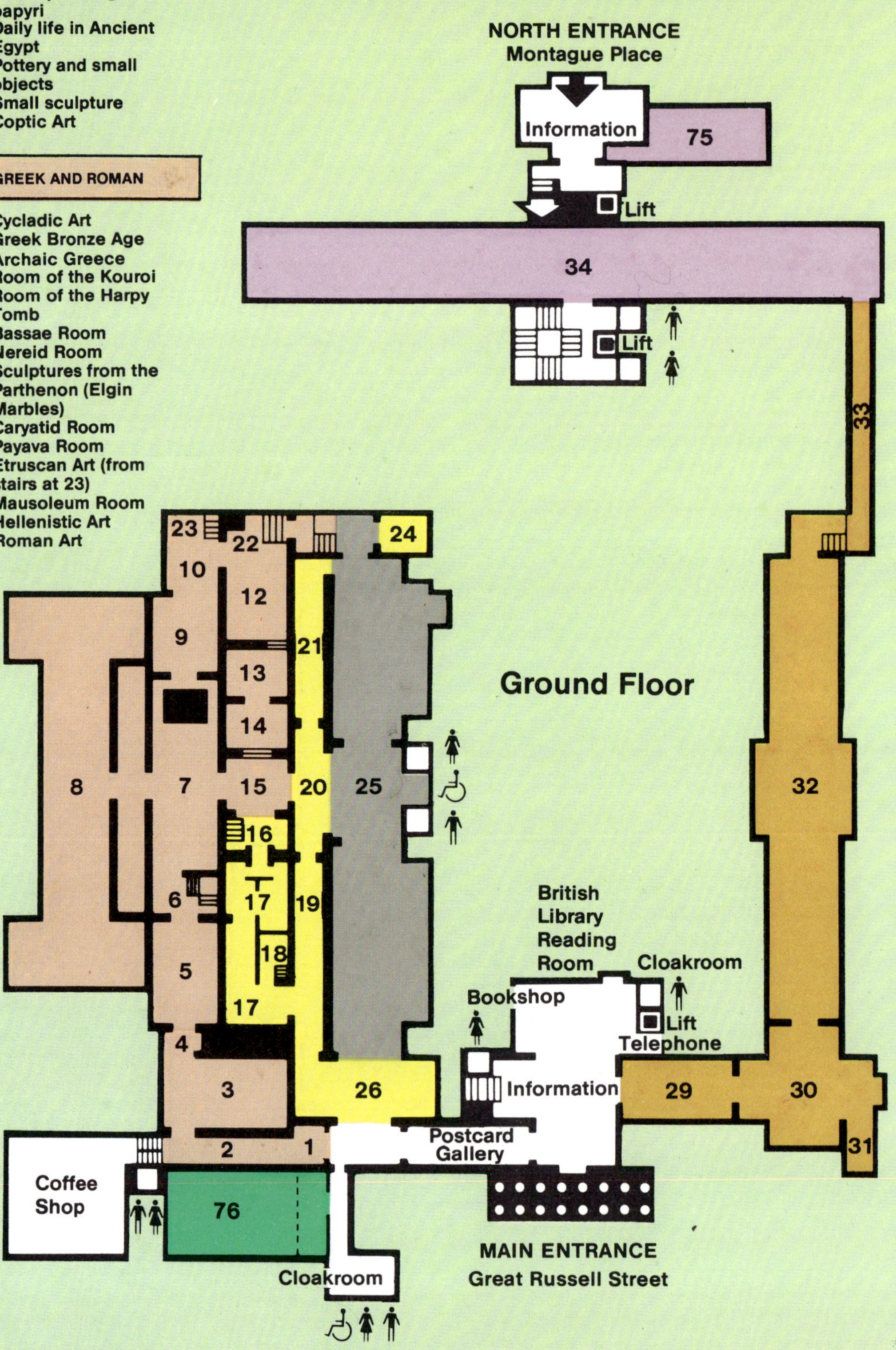

WESTERN ASIATIC

16 Khorsabad, and stairs down to Lecture Theatre
17 Assyrian Saloon
18 Stairs down to Assyrian basement
19/20 Nimrud
21 Nineveh
24 Ancient Palestine
26 Assyrian Transept
51 Ancient Iran
52 Ancient Anatolia
53 Neo-Hittite landing
54 Ancient Babylonia–Royal Tombs of Ur
55 Western Asiatic prehistory
56 Ancient writing
57 Ancient Syria
58 Nimrud Ivories
59 South Arabia

SPECIAL EXHIBITIONS

76 New Wing Gallery
49 Special Exhibitions Gallery

PREHISTORIC AND ROMANO-BRITISH

35 Prehistory and Roman Britain
36 Man before Metals
37/39 Later prehistory of Europe
40 Roman Britain

MEDIEVAL AND LATER

41 Early Medieval Art
42 Medieval Art
43 Medieval tiles and pottery
44 Clocks and watches
45 Waddesdon Bequest
46/47 Renaissance and Later
71 Sutton Hoo Ship Burial*

ORIENTAL

34 Art of Islam, South and South East Asia, China and Korea
74 Oriental Art (special exhibitions only)
75 Art of Japan (lower gallery)

COINS AND MEDALS

50 Coins and Medals Gallery

PRINTS AND DRAWINGS

67 Prints and Drawings

BRITISH LIBRARY GALLERIES

29 Illuminated manuscripts
30 Historical, musical and literary manuscripts
31 Crawford Room
32 King's Library
33 Map Gallery

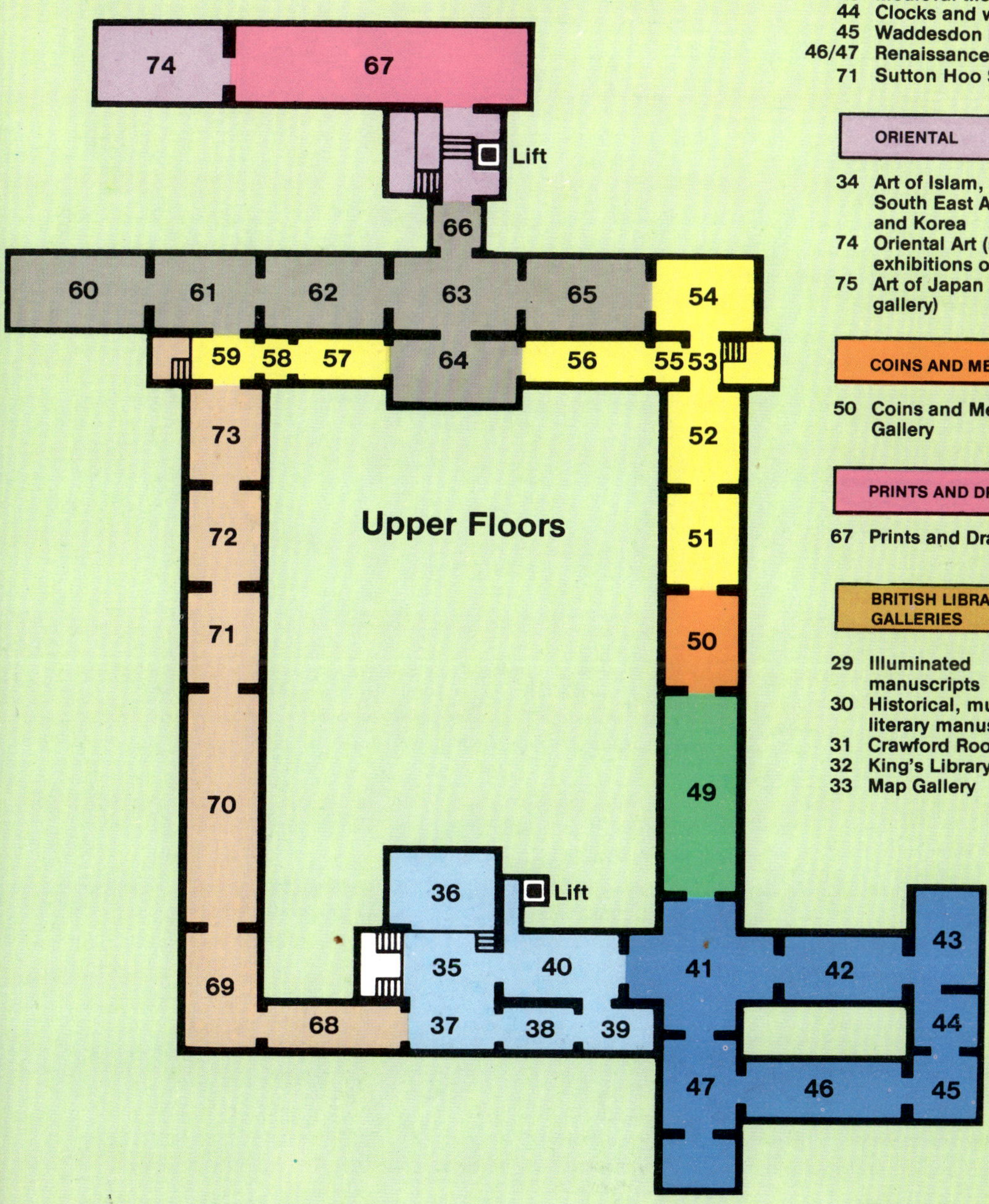

* Temporary display

ORIENTAL ANTIQUITIES

This elegant glazed earthenware tomb figure of a camel (early 8th century AD) is a particularly large and elaborate example from the Tang dynasty, when great attention was paid to detail and features. The piece recalls the animals essential to trade along the Silk Route. Height 84 cm.

The primary galleries of the Department are Oriental Gallery I (room 34), which contains the collections from South and South-east Asia, from the Islamic lands of the Near East, from Central Asia and from the Far East; and Oriental Gallery III (room 75) which contains the Japanese ceramic collections, and is sometimes used for temporary exhibitions. Oriental Gallery II (room 74), apart from the permanent display of a small group of famous sculptures and paintings, is devoted to periodic exhibitions of paintings and prints mainly from Persia, India, China and Japan. The reserve collections, both of antiquities and paintings, are available on application to the Students' Room, from which a student's ticket can be obtained. The Students' Room is open from Monday to Friday 2.15–4.30 and opinions on objects can be given during these hours.

Oriental Gallery I
South and South-east Asia
ROOM 34

The collections, which occupy the west wing of the Gallery, are arranged by cultural province. The visitor is recommended to follow the display in a clockwise direction. The collections from the Indian sub-continent are perhaps the most comprehensive in the West and cover the period from the third millennium BC to the nineteenth century AD. Especially worthy of note are the rich series of Buddhist sculptures from Gandhara (first to sixth centuries AD), among which is the unique Bimaran gold relic casket; the female bracket figure from Sanchi (first century AD); the Buddhist images in stone, bronze, and terracotta panels and gold coins of the Gupta dynasty (fourth to sixth centuries AD); the seated sandstone figure of Ganesa from Western India (tenth century AD); the ivory and wood miniature shrine from Kashmir (eighth century AD); the stone sculptures, Buddhist and Hindu, from Eastern India and Orissa (eighth to twelfth centuries AD), the finest collection outside India; the three female bracket figures (twelfth century AD) and the bronze image of Sarasvati, the goddess of Wisdom (tenth century AD), from the Southern

Deccan; and an outstanding group of stone and bronze images from South India, of which the stone figure of Garuda (about AD 700) and the bronze seated figure of Siva (about AD 950) are masterpieces. The most important sculptures from South-east Asia are the life-size gilt-bronze figure of Tara (ninth to tenth centuries AD); the seated bronze Buddha from Burma (twelfth century AD), and the Raffles Collection of Javanese bronzes (eighth to fourteenth centuries AD).

Oriental Gallery I
Lands of Islam

The Islamic collections, which occupy the west end of the gallery, should also be followed in a clockwise direction. They include pottery, glass, jade, metalwork, and ivories from the eighth to nineteenth centuries AD. Of especial interest are the Hedwig Glass (twelfth century AD); the Mosul inlaid brass ewer (AD 1232); the inlaid brass astrolabe from Cairo (AD 1236); the Syrian enamelled glass pilgrim flask (about AD 1250); the Turkish pottery mosque lamp from Jerusalem (AD 1549); and the large jade tortoise from North India (seventeenth century AD).

Oriental Gallery I
Central Asia

A selection of the antiquities collected by Sir Aurel Stein on his three expeditions to Central Asia are exhibited in the centre of the gallery on the north side.

Oriental Gallery I
China and Korea

The Chinese collections, which occupy the east wing of the gallery, are arranged in chronological order, from the Neolithic

Gandharan Reliquary, **2nd or 3rd century AD. One of the most celebrated objects from the Buddhist world, this splendid gold reliquary set with rubies was found in East Afghanistan. The figures around the sides are the Buddha and gods in attendance. Height 6.7 cm.**

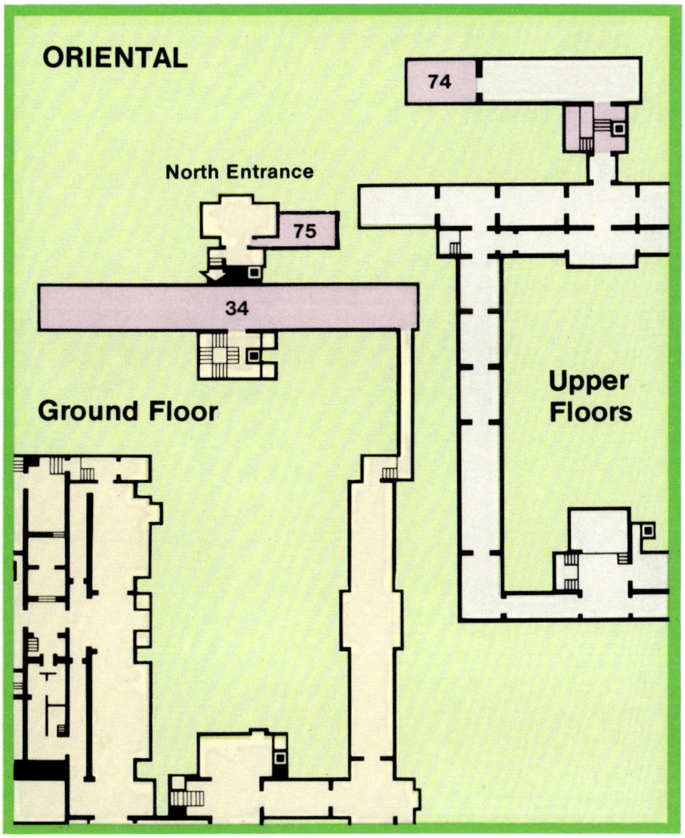

Bronze ritual vessel. *above.* 12th or 11th century BC. This magnificent Shang vessel or *zun*, remarkable for the realism of the two rams which support it, would have been used for holding wine or food in sacrifice. Height 43.2 cm.

period to the Song dynasty (2000 BC–AD 1279) on the south side and east wall, and from the Yuan to the Qing dynasty (AD 1279–1912) on the north. Of especial interest are the bronze ritual vessels and weapons of the Shang and Western Zhou dynasties (1300–700 BC), in particular the famous container formed by two addorsed rams (twelfth-eleventh century BC); the chariot fittings and other ornate bronze of the Eastern Zhou dynasty (500–206 BC), in particular the large bell and two wine vessels (fifth century BC); an early lacquer box of the Han dynasty (206 BC–AD 200); the large pottery tomb figures of the Tang dynasty (AD 618–906); a superlative display of porcelain of the Song dynasty (AD 960–1279), pre-

The poetess Ono No Komachi. *opposite.* This 18th-century print by Harunobu is a fine example of the many Japanese prints in the reserve collections. 27.4 × 20 cm.

Indian bronze god. *below.* c. AD 950. Siva Vishapaharana, swallower of the Poison. Height 59 cm.

鈴木春信画

Porcelain dish. *left.* Early 18th century. Such brightness and variety of colour are characteristic of the Qing dynasty. Diameter 25 cm.

Cloisonné enamel box. *below.* This late 15th-century box displays the extraordinary virtuosity of the Ming enamellers. Diameter 25 cm.

Pilgrim flask. *above left.* c. 1260–1300. A Syrian or Egyptian glass flask richly gilt and enamelled. Height 23 cm, width 21.3 cm.

Pottery dish. *left.* From Iznir (Turkey), 1540–50. These colours are particularly characteristic of the decade. Diameter 39.4 cm.

Figure of a young man. *opposite.* 17th century. Japanese Kakiemon enamelled porcelain such as this was much admired in Europe. Height 30.3 cm.

eminent in which is the phoenix-headed ewer (tenth century AD); the newly-invented under-glaze blue and red decorated porcelain of the Yuan dynasty (AD 1279–1368); the superb blue and white porcelain, carved red lacquer and cloisonné enamels of the first half of the Ming dynasty (AD 1368–1644); and the good collections of porcelain, lacquer and other minor arts of the Qing dynasty (AD 1644–1912). The Korean collections are small but include some Buddhist bronzes of the Great Silla dynasty (AD 668–918), excellent ceramics of the Koryo (AD 918–1392) and Yi (AD 1392–1910) dynasties and one remarkable wooden box decorated with lacquer inlaid with mother-of-pearl and silver wire (thirteenth century AD). There is also a fine group of inlaid and painted lacquer from the Ryukyu Islands (fifteenth to seventeenth centuries AD).

A selection of titles about the Oriental collections available from the Museum Shop:

Ancient China: Art and Archaeology
JESSICA RAWSON

Chinese Porcelain from the Addis Collection
J. M. ADDIS

Chinese Pots 7th-13th Centuries AD
JESSICA RAWSON

Heritage of Tibet
W. ZWALF

Hokusai: Twelve views of Mount Fuji
LAWRENCE SMITH

Japanese Birds and Flowers: twelve album paintings by Kōyō
LAWRENCE SMITH

Japanese Prints: 300 years of albums and books
JACK HILLIER AND LAWRENCE SMITH

Netsuke: The Miniature Sculpture of Japan
RICHARD BARKER AND LAWRENCE SMITH

The Shrines of Gandhara
W. ZWALF

PREHISTORIC AND ROMANO-BRITISH ANTIQUITIES

The Department's collections are drawn from the Paleolithic and Mesolithic periods throughout the world, from the Neolithic, Bronze Age and Iron Age in Europe and from Roman Britain. Limited gallery space allows only part of these collections to be displayed, but students may see reserve collections by appointment. The Prehistory and Roman Britain galleries are on the first floor. At the head of the main stair is the Central Saloon (ROOM 35) which is at present under reorganisation.

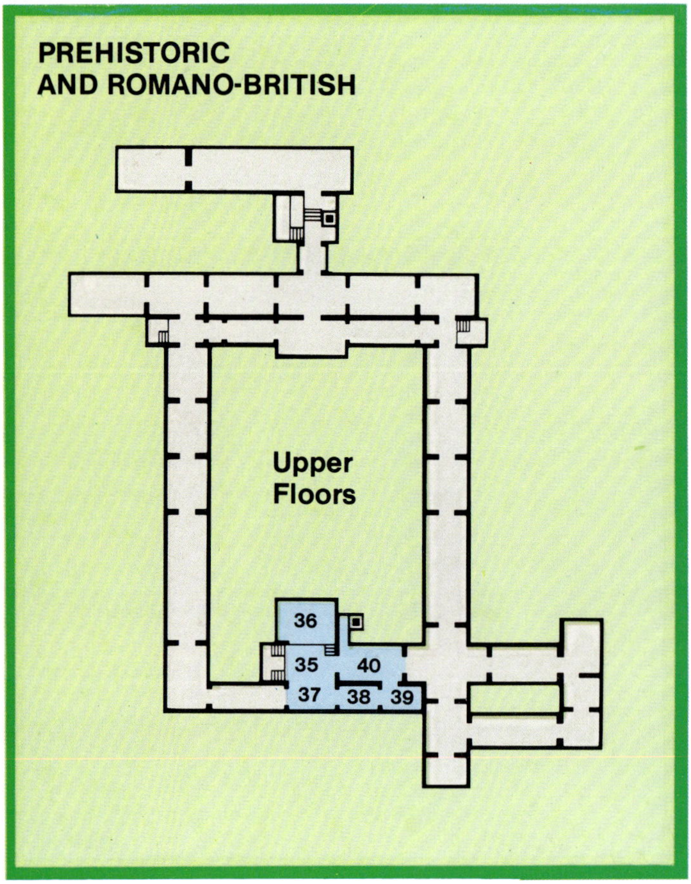

First Prehistory Room

ROOM 36

This houses the 'Man before Metals' display. Here are exhibits spanning the greater part of human prehistory from the emergence of man to his early attempts at metalworking. The crude stone tools from Olduvai Gorge, Tanzania, almost two million years old, can be contrasted with finely worked flint daggers and sickles made in Scandinavia some four thousand years ago; early British pottery can be compared with contemporary European wares; and there is a striking reconstruction of a late Neolithic burial, found at Barnack, Cambridgeshire. However, the highlights of the exhibition are the superb examples of Stone Age art, in particular carvings and figurines in a wide variety of materials. These include the fine Palaeolithic mammoth and reindeer sculptures from Bruniquel, France and an intriguing Neolithic stone figure from the Greek island of Karpathos. On the opposite side of the Central Saloon is the Second Prehistory Room which gives access to two further rooms.

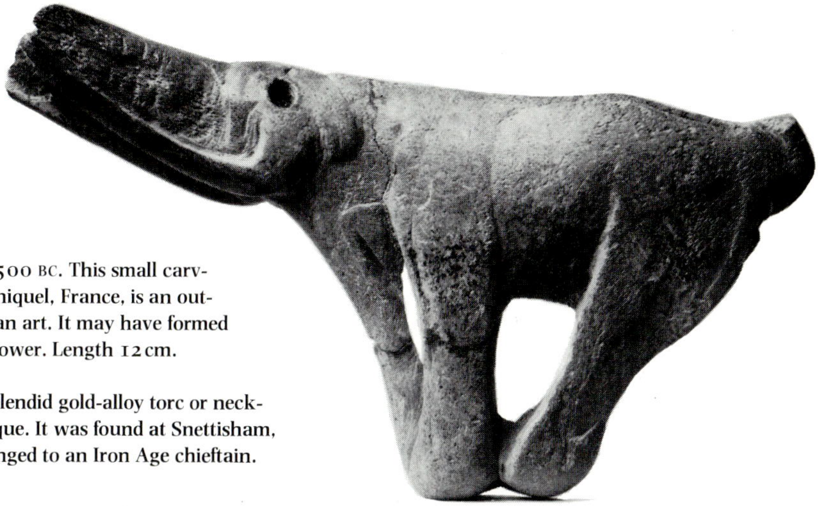

Mammoth. *right.* About 10,500 BC. This small carving in reindeer antler, from Bruniquel, France, is an outstanding example of Magdalenian art. It may have formed part of the handle of a spear-thrower. Length 12 cm.

Electrum torc. *below.* This splendid gold-alloy torc or neck-ring of the 1st century BC is unique. It was found at Snettisham, Norfolk and probably once belonged to an Iron Age chieftain. Diameter 19.6 cm.

Rillaton gold cup. A fine sheet-gold cup (about 1600–1500 BC) from an Early Bronze Age burial in the parish of Linkinhorne, Cornwall. Height 8.5 cm.

Second, Third and Fourth Prehistory Rooms

ROOMS 37/38/39

The exhibits in these three galleries relate to Europe during the last two thousand years BC. They demonstrate the development of both art and technology and hint at the increasing complexity of economic activity and political organisation at this period. Included in the Second Prehistory Room are the contents of some of the rich burials of the British Early Bronze Age, notably the gold cup from Rillaton, Cornwall. In the Third Prehistory Room is a wide range of

Bronze flagon. This magnificent bronze wine flagon, inlaid with coral, is one of a matching pair from Basse-Yutz, Lorraine, France, often called the Lorraine flagons (about 400 BC). They form a fine example of Early Celtic (La Tène) craftsmanship and combine artistic elements of Greek, Oriental and native Hallstatt origin. Height 39 cm.

Bacchus on a tiger. *opposite.* The finely made centre roundel of a once larger mosaic floor (1st or 2nd century AD) found in Leadenhall Street, London, about one hundred metres north-west of the site of the Roman basilica. The scene depicted is of Bacchus reclining on the back of a tiger. As befits the god of wine he wears a wreath of vine leaves, and an empty drinking vessel hangs limply from his right hand. Most of the mosaic cubes are of stone or tile, but the cloak, wreath and staff contain glass cubes in shades of blue and green. Diameter 1.12 m.

Gaming pieces. *below.* These glass counters (about 10 BC–AD 10), from an Iron Age grave at Welwyn Garden City, Hertfordshire, probably belonged to a board game – perhaps a race game like backgammon – requiring four players. There are twenty-four intricately coloured pieces which seem to form a complete set in four colours, six each in white, blue, light green and yellow. A number of amber and glass fragments from the same grave were perhaps used as dice. Diameters 2.5–2.8 cm.

The Witham Shield. *left.* Found in the River Witham, Lincolnshire, this is one of the best surviving examples of Early Celtic fine metalwork from Britain (about 200–100 BC). The thin beaten bronze sheet, with beautifully decorated midrib and bosses originally faced a leather or wooden shield of typical Celtic shape. However it is unlikely to have been intended for active use in warfare. Length 110.4 cm.

British and Continental metalwork showing both the competence of Bronze Age smiths and the importance of trade at this time. To the early Iron Age belong the exquisite Basse-Yutz flagons, seen here with other Classical exports. There is a fine selection of European and British Iron Age pottery in this gallery and the succeeding one, but it is the impressive display of Early Celtic metalwork, especially weapons and jewellery, which dominates the Fourth Prehistory Room. Probably the most famous objects are the shield fronts from the River Witham and from the River Thames at Battersea, and the horned helmet found in the Thames at Waterloo, all made of finely beaten bronze. There is also a dramatic full-scale reconstruction of an Iron Age cremation burial from Welwyn Garden City, Hertfordshire, possibly the tomb of a British chief.

Roman Britain Room

ROOM 40

The objects here date from the period when Britain was a province of the Roman Empire, between the first and early fifth centuries AD. A wide range of exhibits illustrate many aspects of life in the province, both civil and (on the Balcony) military. Perhaps the most spectacular single exhibit is the hoard of fourth century silver tableware from Mildenhall, Suffolk. Equal

Mildenhall platters. These two silver platters of the 4th century AD are examples of the finest work of Roman silversmiths, and are delicately decorated with Bacchic motifs in relief. The top plate shows Pan playing the syrinx (pan-pipes) and a maenad with a double flute, and in the field are a water nymph, a deer, a snake and a covered dish. The other plate shows a satyr and maenad dancing, with various other Bacchic motifs: a syrinx, a skin full of fruit and a covered dish. Diameters 18.8 and 18.5 cm.

Lullingstone wall-plaster. *opposite.* One of six similar figures from a frieze of the 4th century AD which originally graced a room in the Roman villa at Lullingstone, Kent. The outstretched hands indicate that the figure is praying. Height of figure about 70 cm.

in importance are the Vindolanda tablets, the earliest group of written records from Britain. Other major exhibits include the magnificent late Roman treasure from Thetford and the bronze busts of the emperors Claudius and Hadrian. The Water Newton silver, the wall-paintings from Lullingstone, and the Hinton St Mary mosaic pavement are highly significant finds relating to Christianity in Roman Britain.

A selection of titles about the Prehistoric and Romano-British collections available from the Museum Shop:

Arretine and Samian Pottery
CATHERINE JOHNS

Early Celtic Masterpieces from Britain in the British Museum
JOHN BRAILSFORD

Flint Implements

Man before Metals

The Mildenhall Treasure
K. S. PAINTER

Roman Britain
T. W. POTTER

Roman Writing Tablets from Vindolanda
ALAN K. BOWMAN

The Thetford Treasure
JOHNS AND POTTER

The Water Newton Early Christian Silver
K. S. PAINTER

PRINTS AND DRAWINGS

The Department of Prints and Drawings has no permanent exhibition in its gallery on the second floor of the King Edward VII building. Selections from the Department's treasures, usually illustrating a particular theme or school, are, however, normally on display in temporary exhibitions. These exhibitions are usually changed three times a year, and are sometimes varied by loan exhibitions.

The Print Room of the British Museum contains one of the great collections of European prints and drawings. The series of woodcuts, engravings and etchings, from their beginnings in the early fifteenth century down to modern times, is as representative as any in existence, and includes almost complete series of the engravings and etchings of, amongst others, Schongauer, Durer, Lucas van Leyden and Rembrandt. The collection of drawings consists of all European schools from the fifteenth century onwards. The representation of the English school is naturally the largest and at present includes 20,000 drawings from the Turner Bequest, deposited on indefinite loan by the Trustees of the National Gallery. But all the greatest European artists are represented, in many cases superbly: among the highlights of the collection are groups of drawings by Michelangelo, Raphael, Dürer, Rubens, Rembrandt, Claude Lorrain and

above. **Sandro Botticelli** (1444–1510), ***Abundance*** **or** ***Autumn, c.*** **1480. Drawing in pen and brown ink and wash, heightened with white, on pink prepared paper. 31 × 44.7 cm.**

opposite above. **Thomas Girtin** (1775–1802), **Westminster from Lambeth: study for the** ***Panorama of London, c.*** **1800. Watercolour. 29.2 × 52 cm.**

opposite below. **Rembrandt** (1606–69), ***The Three Trees,*** **1643. Etching. 21.1 × 28 cm.**

Watteau. The Students' Room is adjacent to the Exhibition Gallery and is open to students who wish to study prints and drawings not on exhibition. Ticket holders are admitted from Monday to Friday, 10 a.m. to 1 p.m., and 2.15 to 4 p.m.; Saturdays 10 a.m. to 12.30 p.m. Members of the public may make enquiries or seek opinions on Monday to Friday, 2.15 to 4 p.m.; Saturdays 10 a.m. to 12.30 p.m.

Many books on the collections of the Prints and Drawings department are available at the bookshop, including:

Drawings by Michelangelo
J. A. GERE

Goya's Prints
JULIET WILSON BAREAU

Italian Baroque Drawings
NICHOLAS TURNER

Looking at Drawings: a guide to technical terms
PAUL GOLDMAN

Looking at Prints: a guide to technical terms
PAUL GOLDMAN

Prints and Printmaking: an introduction to the history and techniques
ANTONY GRIFFITHS

Rubens: Drawings and Sketches
JOHN ROWLANDS

Turner in the British Museum: Drawings and Watercolours
ANDREW WILTON

WESTERN ASIATIC ANTIQUITIES

The Department includes antiquities of the Sumerians, Babylonians, and Assyrians, from what is now Iraq; the ancient Persians, including the Parthians and Sassanians; the Urartians and the Hittites, who extended from Turkey into northern Syria; other peoples of Syria and ancient Palestine, including the Phoenicians with their colonies as far afield as Carthage; and all the states of the Arabian peninsula, especially North and South Yemen.

The period covered is from the earliest agricultural settlements, roughly 7000 BC, until the advent of Islam in the seventh century AD.

Our evidence for the history of this area down to about 3500 BC derives largely from the remains of small villages. From then on we have evidence of bigger towns and states, associated with the development of written documents, especially in Iraq and southern Iran. The rich culture of the Sumerians, about 2500 BC, is attested by finds from the 'Royal Cemetery' at Ur. The political history of the next two thousand years is highly complicated; most of what we know derives from clay tablets in the cuneiform script. During this time a series of empires developed and disintegrated in turn. One of the most powerful was the Assyrian empire which, in the seventh century BC, controlled territory from Egypt to Iran, and from Anatolia into Arabia; the Assyrian sculptures illustrate events at this time. The Babylonian empire which succeeded the Assyrian was replaced in the late sixth century BC by the Achaemenian Persian empire, which united almost all of western Asia. Alexander the Great destroyed the Persian dominion, in the late fourth century BC, but his conquests came to be divided among various successor states. Eventually the western areas fell under Roman and then Byzantine control, while the east formed part of the Parthian and Sassanian empires, both based in Persia. Some of these great powers had flourishing trade relations with the South Arabian kingdoms of Yemen, but the latter remained for the most part politically independent.

The Department's collections derive mainly from archaeological expeditions sponsored by the British Museum. The Assyrian sculptures were mostly discovered by Layard and Rassam in the mid-nineteenth century. The same two men excavated the bulk of the vast collection of cuneiform tablets from Assyria and Babylonia. Among the most important discoveries of the twentieth century are those made by Woolley at Ur.

The Black Obelisk. **Assyrian stone obelisk, about 825 BC, with carvings that show Shalmaneser, king of Assyria, receiving tribute from various foreign rulers including Jehu, king of Israel. From Nimrud (north Iraq). Height 202 cm.**

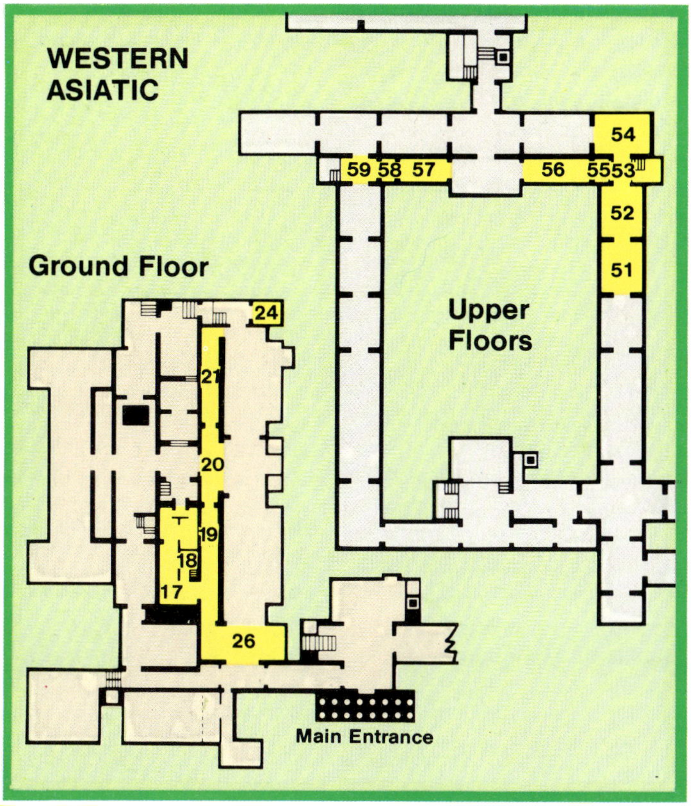

Assyrian Transept
ROOM 26

Colossal human-headed winged lion and bull from the palace of Ashurnasirpal II (883–859 BC) at Nimrud. A free-standing statue of Ashurnasirpal from one of the Nimrud temples, and other sculptures from Nimrud and elsewhere. Sets of bronze gates, notably the bronze gates of Shalmaneser III (858–824 BC) from Balawat, showing Assyrian victories, processions of tribute-bearers and other scenes of Assyrian life.

Nimrud Gallery
ROOM 19

Sculptures from the palace of Ashurnasirpal at Nimrud. Most of the panels on the west wall come from the royal throne-room, and show hunting or military scenes. Those on the east wall show the king, his courtiers, and various magical figures which were thought to protect the building. In the centre of the gallery is a statue of Shalmaneser III, from the Assyrian religious capital of Ashur, and the Black Obelisk of Shalmaneser III, from Nimrud, which shows in the second row the tribute of Jehu, king of Samaria, about 841 BC.

Nimrud Central Saloon
ROOM 20

Sculptures of Tiglath-pileser III (745–727 BC) from Nimrud. These show the king's conquests in Babylonia and Syria.

Khorsabad Entrance
ROOM 16

Sculptures of Sargon (722–705 BC). Colossal human-headed winged bulls from a citadel gate at Khorsabad. A panel showing a bird-hunt. On one wall a paving slab carved with floral decoration as a carpet.

Assyrian Saloon
ROOM 17

Sculptures of Sennacherib (704–681 BC) and Ashurbanipal (668–*c.* 627 BC), from Nineveh. A series of panels from Sennacherib's palace, showing his attack on the city of Lachish in Palestine in 701 BC, the fall of the city, and the fate of the in-

Ashurnasirpal II (883–859 BC). This Assyrian stone statue showing the king who founded the Assyrian empire was originally placed in a temple at Kalhu (Biblical Calah), his capital city. The king is wearing ritual dress, and carries in his left hand a mace symbolising his authority. From Nimrud (north Iraq). Height 113 cm.

habitants. Panels showing the horses of Sennacherib, and Ashurbanipal's lions in a garden. Several series of Ashurbanipal's Hunts: shooting lions from his chariot and killing them while on foot or riding a horse; chasing onagers with hounds and ambushing gazelle; the march out to the hunt, and the return.

Assyrian Basement

ROOM 18

Sculptures showing the wars of Ashurbanipal in Iran, Arabia, Babylonia, and Egypt, and his celebrations after victory. Broken Assyrian obelisks. Armour and objects of daily life from Assyria. The Ishtar Temple procession. History of early excavation in Assyria. A column-base from Persepolis (Iran).

Nineveh Gallery

ROOM 21

Sculptures from the palace of Sennacherib at Nineveh. The transport of a colossal winged bull. Battles in the marshes. The White Obelisk (Ashurnasirpal).

Ancient Palestine Room

ROOM 24

Reconstruction of a rock-cut tomb from Jericho. Pottery and jewellery. The ossuary of Nicanor. Coins of the Jewish states.

Human-headed winged bull. **Assyrian, about 710 BC. This colossal stone slab was originally placed beside a gate in a city built by the Assyrian king, Sargon II. From Khorsabad (north Iraq). Length 486cm.**

Ascending the North-West Staircase, the visitor reaches the

South Arabian Landing

ROOM 59

Bronzes and sculptures from North and South Yemen (last centuries BC to first centuries AD).

Ivory Room

ROOM 58

A display of ivory carvings, mainly from Nimrud (ninth to seventh centuries BC), in various styles. The plaque showing a lioness killing a negro: Phoenician workmanship with Egyptian influence.

Syrian Room

ROOM 57

Syrian and Phoenician antiquities from the second millennium BC to the Roman period. The statue of Idrimi. Sculptures from Tell Halaf. Phoenician bronzework from Nimrud and jewellery from the colony of Tharros in Sardinia. Tombstones from the Phoenician (Punic) city of Carthage in Tunisia. Portrait heads from the cemeteries at Palmyra, the trading city in the Syrian desert.

Beyond the Sixth Egyptian Room is the

Room of Writing

ROOM 56

The early history of writing illustrated by documents in cuneiform and alphabetic scripts. The library of Ashurbanipal: the Flood Tablet. Seals used on clay tablets.

Prehistoric Room

ROOM 55

The beginnings of agriculture and urbanisation in Western Asia (7000–3000 BC), illustrated by pottery and other small objects.

Ashurbanipal feasting. *above.* Detail from one of the stone panels (about 645 BC) that decorated the state apartments in the palace of Ashurbanipal, the last great king of Assyria. The king reclines on a couch in his garden, accompanied by his queen, while musicians play nearby. From Nineveh (north Iraq). Height 56 cm.

Dying lioness. *below.* Detail from the stone panelling of Ashurbanipal's palace (about 645 BC). This animal is one of several that were shot by the Assyrian king in an arena. Shooting lions was a favourite Assyrian royal sport, and the events were represented with memorable artistry. From Nineveh (north Iraq). Width 75 cm.

Across the Hittite Landing, and to the left, is the

Babylonian Room

ROOM 54

Antiquities illustrating the arts and daily life of the Sumerians and Babylonians. Objects discovered in the 'Royal Cemetery' at Ur (about 2500 BC); the 'Standard of Ur', with mosaic scenes of war and peace; the goat in a thicket; a harp and lyres; reconstruction of a royal sledge; elaborate jewellery; weapons and vessels. Decoration of a Sumerian temple at Al-Ubaid (about 2500 BC).

Hittite Landing

ROOM 53

Sculptures from Carchemish tenth to eighth centuries BC.

Anatolian Room

ROOM 52

Antiquities from Turkey. Hittite jewellery from Carchemish. Standard from Alaca Huyuk (about 2500 BC). Urartian bronzes from Toprak Kale (eighth to seventh centuries BC).

Iranian Room

ROOM 51

Antiquities from the third millennium BC to the seventh century AD. Elamite culture. Bronzes from Luristan. Achaemenian art, including the Oxus Treasure goldwork and the glazed brick archer from Susa. Parthian and Sassanian culture.

Goat and tree. *above.* **This Sumerian statue, made about 2500 BC, was originally one of a pair that probably supported a small table. From the Royal Cemetery at Ur (south Iraq). Height 45.7 cm.**

Lion killing a negro. *left.* **Phoenician, about 8th century BC. An ivory plaque, originally one of a pair, probably from a piece of furniture. From Nimrud (north Iraq). Height 10.2 cm.**

A selection of titles about the Western Asiatic collections available from the Museum Shop:

Ancient Bronzes from Luristan
P. R. S. MOOREY

Assyrian Sculpture
JULIAN READE

The Babylonian Legend of the Flood
E. SOLLBERGER

Illustrations of Old Testament History
R. D. BARNETT

The Nimrud Ivories
MAX MALLOWAN

Golden armlet. Achaemenian, about 5th century BC. One of a pair of ceremonial armlets, once elaborately inlaid, which belonged to the so-called Oxus Treasure. The animals are griffins, monsters which frequently appear in the art of the Persian Empire. From Russian Turkestan. Diameter 12.7cm.

The Flood Tablet. This clay tablet, written in the cuneiform script in the 7th century BC, is one of the large number of texts collected by the Assyrian king, Ashurbanipal, for his palace library. It tells a story, part of the Epic of Gilgamesh, which bears some striking resemblances to the Biblical story of Noah's ark. The hero of the Akkadian version of the Flood story is called Uta-napishtim; he was eventually granted immortality, and recounted the story of the Flood to Gilgamesh, who had come in search of immortality for himself. From Nineveh (north Iraq). Height 13.7cm.

MUSEUM OF MANKIND ETHNOGRAPHY

Central African figure. *above.* This wood-carving, one of a series made to commemorate former kings of the Bakuba people of Zaire, represents a 17th-century ruler, identified by the gaming board at his feet. Height 54 cm.

Nigerian 'bronze' head. *right.* Cast by the 'lost wax' technique, this 16th-century head of a Queen Mother was made to stand on an ancestral altar. Height 39 cm. (Photo by David Finn)

The Museum of Mankind, in Burlington Gardens near Piccadilly, houses the British Museum's Ethnography Department. Here a number of regularly changing exhibitions illustrate a wide variety of non-Western societies and cultures. The Museum's enormous collections derive from the indigenous peoples of Africa, Australia and the Pacific Islands, North and South America and some areas of Europe and Asia. Various ancient as well as recent and contemporary cultures are represented. In order to display this material in the depth it deserves, most exhibitions concentrate on the way of life of particular peoples or on specific aspects of culture, arts and technologies. In addition, however, a selection from the Museum's finest artistic treasures is constantly on display. Of necessity most of the collections must be kept in store where they await future exhibitions and are made available to researchers and serious students.

It is impossible to give more than a very brief description of the Museum's collections here, but a few of the most important may be mentioned. The artistic traditions of many parts of Africa are particu-

West African gown. **A gown from the Mandingo of Liberia, made from strips of cotton cloth woven on a narrow loom. The cloth is dyed in different shades of indigo and decorated with embroidery and appliqué. Height 93 cm.**

larly well represented, in pottery, textiles and other media as well as in sculpture. Perhaps the most spectacular are the 'bronze' work and carved ivories from Benin in Nigeria, but other remarkable collections include gold regalia from the kingdom of Asante in Ghana and fine woodcarvings from West and Central Africa. Personal ornaments are an important feature of collections from other parts of the continent.

From the Pacific come the artefacts of Australia's Aboriginal people and the elaborate religious art of the Melanesian Islands. The sculpture of New Guinea is especially well represented, including a recently acquired painted and carved men's sacred house from the Sepik area. Objects from the Polynesian islands are also particularly important, especially the large number of rare religious images, and many pieces derive from the voyages of the earliest European explorers such as Captain Cook.

Much of the Museum's most ancient material comes from Middle and South America, for all the indigenous cultures of the Americas, archaeological and recent, fall within its scope. Finely decorated pottery and textiles from ancient burials dominate the Peruvian collections, and among other things there is gold from Colombia and important examples of architectural sculpture from the Maya area. Among the most striking objects from the ancient civilisations of the Americas are the Aztec-period mosaic masks from Mexico, covered in minute pieces of polished turquoise and other semi-precious stones, and the magnificent jadeite ceremonial adze from the ancient Olmec culture.

More recent American Indian cultures from both South and North America are represented, for instance, by the elaborate feather ornaments of the tropical forest tribes, the embroidered hide costumes of the North American Plains and the fine ivory carvings of the Eskimoes. From the North Pacific Coast a rich tradition of woodcarving is represented by masks, ritual objects and the well known 'totem poles'.

European and Asian collections at the Museum of Mankind complement the predominantly fine art collections of other British Museum departments. These parts of the world are mainly represented by the arts, crafts and technology of peasant and tribal communities. The most important collections from the Middle East are textiles, weaving apparatus and costumes from the Bedouin of Jordan, the villagers of Palestine and the nomads of Baluchistan. From central India there is a fine collection with tools and agricultural implements from the Gonds, and from Assam there are the finely ornamented ceremonial costumes and weapons of the Naga hill tribes. From the north there are the

New Guinea shield. *left above.* **A shield from the central highlands of New Guinea, carved from a single piece of wood and coloured with charcoal, lime and ochre. Height 151 cm.**

New Guinea mask. *left.* **Masks like this, of painted barkcloth on a cane frame, were made by the coastal people of the Papuan Gulf area to impersonate forest spirits in annual festivals. Height 165 cm.**

Tahiti mourner's costume. *opposite.* **This costume, collected on Captain Cook's second voyage, was worn to terrorise the people following the death of a chief. Height 220 cm.**

North American Indian frontlet. *above.* A frontlet representing a mythological raven and worn on the front of a ceremonial headdress on the Northwest Coast. Height 27 cm.

Peruvian pottery figure. *right.* Vessels like this, which represents a warrior, were buried with the dead by the prehistoric Moche people of Peru. Height 21 cm.

Mexican mosaic mask. *opposite.* This Aztec-period mask, carved from wood and covered with turquoise, is thought to represent the god Quetzalcoatl and may have been given to Cortes, the Conqueror of Mexico. Height 17 cm.

Hawaiian Bowl. *below.* A carved bowl, used by Hawaiian chiefs for kava, a mildly narcotic drink. Length 51 cm.

artefacts of the reindeer herding and hunting peoples from Lappland to Siberia, and the diverse cultures of South-east Asia are particularly well represented. Especially rich are the collections formed by Sir Stamford Raffles, nineteenth-century Lieutenant-Governor of Java, with intricately pierced and painted shadow puppets, theatrical masks and *gamelan* orchestra.

In addition to fine artistic works, the Museum also con-

tains an immense variety of less spectacular objects which are equally important in illustrating the ways of life of the peoples who made and used them. All types of everyday tools and utensils are represented; household equipment and furnishings, costume and personal possessions, religious paraphernalia and weapons. Together these collections enable the Museum to illustrate in depth a variety of human societies and cultures, most of which have been drastically transformed in recent times.

Besides its exhibitions, the Museum of Mankind's services include a regular free programme of anthropological film shows. Staff are available to answer enquiries and one of the largest anthropological libraries in the world is open to those wishing to pursue research. The stores, in London's East End, are also open to researchers by appointment, while the Education Service helps schools and the general public make use of the Museum's less specialised resources. Further details of these services and of the current exhibitions are available from the Museum of Mankind.

A selection of titles about the ethnographic collections available from the Museum Shop:

African Textiles
JOHN PICTON AND JOHN MACK

The Asante
M. D. MCLEOD

Malay Shadow Puppets
AMIN SWEENEY

Moche Pottery from Peru
GEORGE BANKES

Textiles of Baluchistan
M. G. KONIECZNY

The Tribal Image: Wooden Figure Sculpture of the World
WILLIAM FAGG

Javanese shadow puppet. *above.* Such puppets, cut from parchment, painted and gilded, represent characters from Hindu epics. This one is part of the collection of Sir Stamford Raffles. Height 85 cm.

Central African raffia cloth. *above right.* Cloth, decorated with cut-pile embroidery, made by the Bakuba of Zaire for display at funerals.

Palestinian dress. *right.* The Arab women of Palestine make these dresses from locally-woven linen which they embroider with intricate designs in coloured silks. Height 139 cm.

North American Indian carving. *opposite.* A carving of a mother and child which was made by the Nootka people of the Northwest Coast and collected on Captain Cook's voyage of 1778. Height 27 cm.

THE BRITISH LIBRARY

The British Library was established in July 1973 under an Act of Parliament, by bringing together the library departments of the British Museum (including the National Reference Library for Science and Invention) to form the Reference Division, and various other national organisations to create a Lending Division, a Bibliographic Services Division and also a Research and Development Department.

Two of the departments of the Reference Division, the Department of Printed Books and the Department of Manuscripts, are still based in the British Museum building. Admission to the reading rooms is by reader's pass which may be applied for at the Reader Admissions Office, just off the main hall of the Museum. However, the magnificent domed Reading Room, which has been in use since 1857, may be viewed by visitors on the hour, every hour, from 11 a.m. to 4 p.m.

Some Treasures of the British Library

The Reference Division constitutes one of the world's greatest libraries, with its more than ten million volumes and many hundreds of thousands of manuscripts, maps, music scores, periodicals, newspapers and the philatelic collections. A selection of treasures comprising illuminated manuscripts, both Western and Oriental, historical manuscripts and books illustrating the history of printing, fine book binding and book illustration, is always on display in the three galleries which can be entered from the right of the main hall. In sequence they are the Grenville Library, the Manuscript Saloon and the King's Library. There are also regular special exhibitions on particular themes. On the floor above, in the gallery leading to the Museum's Oriental galleries, is a changing selection of exhibitions from the Map Room.

Among the most famous items on permanent display are:

Magna Carta. Two of the four surviving copies of the charter issued in 1215 by King John, enshrining his agreement with his barons which had been sealed at Runnymede a few days before.

The Lindisfarne Gospels. One of England's greatest masterpieces of book painting, this was written and illuminated about 698 by Eadfrith, Bishop of Lindisfarne.

Shakespeare's First Folio. The first publication in 1623 of Shakespeare's collected works.

The Gutenberg Bible. The first book to be printed using movable metal type, *c.* 1453.

The Lindisfarne Gospels. *opposite.* **Decorative 'cross-carpet' page preceding the Gospel according to Saint Luke (Cotton MS Nero D. iv, folio 139).**

The Lindisfarne Gospels is beyond question the outstanding masterpiece of English book illumination. The manuscript was written and illuminated in the island monastery of Lindisfarne, off the coast of Northumbria, probably to mark the translation of the relics of Saint Cuthbert there in 698. The artist, a monk named Eadfrith, was shortly afterwards elected Bishop. In the design of his pages, Eadfrith displays a mastery of the Anglo-Saxon love of ornament, blending his many separate motifs into a satisfying entity with apparently effortless ease.

INDEX

ISBN 0-7141-2011-1

Printing 1 3456789
Published by British Museum Publications Limited
46 Bloomsbury Street
London WC1B 3QQ
Designed by Roger Davies
Maps drawn by Roger Davies
Set in Monophoto Photina
Printed in Great Britain by
Jolly & Barber Ltd, Rugby.